360°
IMPACT

A Guide to Live,
Lead, and Serve in a More
Colorful World!

MICHELE KLINE

ISBN: 978-1-964619-08-8

Table of Contents

Foreword

The following pages are the result of a collaborative effort from individuals who embody the power of genuine connection, compassionate leadership, and the mastery of communication. Their unwavering support, profound wisdom, and pivotal roles in my life and leadership journey have been indispensable in the creation of this book. Their insights and experiences have not only molded me as a leader but have also significantly fueled the passion and vision behind this project. Their perspectives infuse this book with a unique and cherished essence, reflecting the true spirit of living, leading, and serving with impact.

"The greatest leaders we've ever known – at work, at home, or in our communities - share a simple, yet profound ability to make a positive IMPACT on everyone around them. Great leaders are not great because of their "leadershipness"; great leaders are great because of their *humanness*. Michele Kline has written '*360° IMPACT*' as a call to action for all of us to lean into our *humanness*. She reminds us that being a great leader isn't limited to our professional lives. Instead, happier, healthier, more joyful, and much more fulfilling life experiences are attainable for anyone willing to accept the challenge of becoming an inspiration to others at work, at home, and in our communities.

Thank you, Michele, for showing us how to lean into our own *Growth, Gratitude, Purpose, Connection, Integration,* and *Collaboration* to make a 360-degree impact wherever we go in this incredibly colorful life we get to live." - **Taylor Scott, author of *Ballgames to Boardrooms* and *Lead with Hospitality*, The Founder and President of Lead with Hospitality, LLC**

"It is with great pleasure that I introduce *"360° IMPACT,"* authored by my dear friend Michele, whose wisdom and insights have inspired me over our sixteen-year journey together. In her book, you will take a deep dive and explore yourself, both personally and professionally, across six transformative chapters. Each chapter will build on the next as you explore yourself in self-discovery, offering insights and practical strategies to empower yourself along your life journey. From understanding the fundamentals to overcoming challenges like imposter syndrome to nurturing emotional intelligence and fostering meaningful connections, this book provides a roadmap for navigating both personal and professional spheres. It's a testament to our enduring friendship and my friend's dedication to empowering others. May these chapters inspire you to embrace growth, purpose, and collaboration as you navigate your own path in life." - **Melissa Aarskaug, Vice President Gaming at Bulletproof, a Gaming Laboratories International LLC company. Founder & Voice of The Executive Connect (a podcast that produces industry-leading content for organizational leaders looking to sharpen their skills)**

"As humans, we are all interconnected by an invisible field. The way we nurture these connections can turn our lives and our surroundings into either a source of exhaustion or a beautiful haven. This book is a heartfelt guide to finding the paths to live, work, and cherish life while making a difference for the sake of all.

From a tender age, Michele showed a natural inclination to help others. In school, she often stood up for her classmates, sometimes at a personal cost. As life has unfolded, her experiences and the inner work she has done have called her to once again share her wisdom. She is here to help us connect in new, meaningful ways to face the challenges of our evolving world together." - **Silvia Castex, Architect & Interior Designer**

"It was the mid 2000's when I first met Michele Kline and I was immediately struck by her drive. *"That lady knows what she wants... and gets it..."* I thought. 20 years later, the book you are holding, her latest masterpiece, depicts an inspiring journey of "clarity, drive and purpose" and the ingredients for leadership through human connection with a *"360° IMPACT"*.

I am confident these strategies will transcend into your life as much as they have in mine. Enjoy!" - **Ana Rodriguez-Kilby, Organizational Effectiveness Expert**

"This book is the ultimate tool for learning, enjoyment, and winning. A boss is obeyed, but a leader is followed—a beacon in a stormy night. God has blessed Michele with remarkable intelligence. Her dedication to studying the works of influential thinkers has given her a profound education, and her successful career has endowed her with invaluable experience. She is now sharing all of this with you in her book.

Her motto, 'win or learn,' reflects her commitment to continuous growth and extraordinary resilience." - **Dr. Jorge Castex, Doctor of Juridical Science & Corporate Attorney**

"As a speaker, trainer, and leadership facilitator with over two decades of experience, I recognize the urgent need for effective leaders in today's rapidly evolving world. In 360° IMPACT, A Guide to Live, Lead, and Serve in a More Colorful World, Michele provides a timely and relevant guide to navigating the complexities of modern leadership with the white glove approach of hospitality.

Michele uncovered the key to unlocking my potential, transforming my approach to leadership – at work and at play - empowering me to take the forefront with confidence. Explore your personal leadership journey with thought provoking questions, practical application, and Michele as your guide. Drawing from Michele's gift of cultivating leaders, prepare to be inspired and empowered to become the leader you are destined to be." - **Janice T Tanaka, Keynote Speaker, Vocal Empowerment Trainer, Leadership Facilitator JT Training and Consulting, LLC**

"From a young age, we all develop daily habits—whether it's brushing our teeth, tying our shoes, or preparing for the day ahead. Similarly, Michele has cultivated daily rituals and habits that enable her to become the best version of herself, ultimately to positively impact you. Michele's passion is not only evident in her book but also in every interaction of her daily life. She inspires us all through her writing, reminding us of the simple tasks and actions that lead to greatness or small improvements that just make good sense." - **Mark Kline, Regional Manager Enterprise at Cisco Systems, Inc.**

Introduction

There are three things that are a must for me when I meet someone: creating a genuine connection, serving them in some way, and opening a door to discovering where they plan to go next in life.

Since I was very young, as my parents often recount, I have shown leadership qualities. Constantly seeking ways to connect with people on a deeper level. Although this sometimes feels "weird" or "uncomfortable" for some people, I have found my way around it, whether by focusing on improving the dialogue *(fun fact: I find gossip as appealing as pineapple on pizza, no offense intended)* or seeking a setting that aligns with my aspiration for growth.

Throughout my life, I have remained dedicated to positively impacting my community—even when my mother would occasionally grow frustrated with me for being "too altruistic," as it would sometimes get me in trouble—whether through involvement in philanthropic endeavors, offering perspective when it was most needed, lending a hand to those around me, or helping people navigate challenging situations.

As an advocate for the environment, I remember being about nine years old and offering my mother all my savings to register me to become a supporting member of Greenpeace. Although I did not know much about the organization, I knew they were making an impact on the environment, at least from the perspective from which I received the information (be mindful that the World Wide Web was not invented until 1989, and it took a few years before this phenomenon would reach any typical household). I also knew that every month, I would receive a super cool copy of their magazine, where they showcased the impact they were making on a global level, and this gave me a sense of belonging to something big and in perfect alignment with my desire to heal the world.

[*Greenpeace is an independent global campaigning network, founded in Canada in 1971 by a group of environmental activists.]

Why engage in philanthropy, environmental advocacy, and speaking up for others? Why did I undertake all these efforts? I do not believe it is because leadership is an innate skill, but because I had then, *as I do now*, an unwavering desire to leave this world better than I found it.

I have come to realize that engaging with others on a deeper level and inspiring them to adopt a positive mindset not only brings me immense joy, but it is also the answer that we as humans lack.

It saddens me to share that we have forgotten how to genuinely connect!

As you choose to continue to read this book, I invite you to explore a subject that does not just rock the boat but steers it with purpose: *"Connecting with yourself and with people to create a 360° IMPACT."*

We all strive to enhance the outcomes in our lives, whether it is financial gains, more time, a different lifestyle, inspiring relationships, or better health. What I have learned is that to truly impact our own lives and those of the people around us, we must excel at connecting with people. Because no human can thrive in isolation; we rely on each other.

> *Regardless of who you are, you can amplify your impact by honing your ability to connect.*

So, what is human connection?

It is the invisible thread that weaves our hearts together, transcending physical proximity and reaching into the depths of our souls. It is the profound resonance we feel when our spirits recognize each other within the limitlessness of existence.

> *Like stars scattered across the night sky,*
> *each individual carries a unique light, and through connection,*
> *these lights can shine in harmony.*

Human connection is a dance of empathy and understanding. It is the art of truly seeing and being seen, of listening with not just our ears but with our hearts. It is a shared vulnerability, a willingness to open ourselves to another, revealing the raw beauty of our innermost selves without fear of judgment.

Human connection is also a fragile miracle, easily obscured by the noise of modern life. It requires presence and intentionality, moments of undivided attention in the chaos, where time slows down and souls touch.

Why do we rarely make *(key word)* the time to pause, unwind, or escape the constant noise? And if we occasionally do, why is this not habitual?

Think about this for a moment. You want to enhance your marriage? The key lies in fostering moments to genuinely connect with your spouse. Do you want to communicate better with your children, your parents, or your siblings? Connection bridges this gap. Seeking a promotion at work? Building a strong connection with your boss is essential. Aiming to increase sales? Connecting authentically with your customers is the way forward. Dreaming of cultivating a culture of trust, respect, and teamwork within your organization? It starts with improving your ability to connect with your team. Looking to deepen your friendships? Well, you know the answer, you must strengthen those connections!

Genuinely connecting is not a walk in the park. But if I can convince you that connection is all about turning every interaction into an avenue for powerful engagement, you are already a step ahead.

You see, there is an epidemic. People have jumped onto the "busy wagon" and have forgotten about the power of human connection. The genuine connection that can alleviate your relentless and demanding sense of "busy".

We forgot that all the people we interact with are human!

Your customers are not just transactions; they are human beings with needs, desires, and emotions. The lady at the register is not simply processing a sale; she is a person with her own experiences and perspectives. Your suppliers are more than just business contacts; they are individuals working to support their families and livelihoods. Your team members are not just employees; they are human beings with aspirations and challenges of their own. And when it comes to your children, your siblings, parents, and spouse, they rely on you for guidance, support, and love.

All these interactions are fundamentally human. They are built on trust, empathy, and understanding. Recognizing the humanity in everyone we encounter, whether it is a customer, a colleague, a family member, or a friend, is essential to fostering genuine connections and building meaningful relationships. When we acknowledge and honor the humanity in others, we cultivate trust and respect, laying the foundation for mutual support and collaboration. And this is what genuine connection is all about!

The question now becomes, *how*, *when*, and most importantly, *why* did we forget about the impact that connection can have on our lives?

In my humble opinion, those who learn the skill of connection discover a profound edge.

What I have also come to realize over the years is that impactful leadership can be learned. I strongly believe that leadership is a choice! And even for those for whom these traits may come easy, they must ALWAYS keep learning, keep sharpening their skills, and keep striving for excellence in this realm.

Over the past 25 years, I have found myself presented with the chance to lead many teams. Incredible humans from all kinds of backgrounds.

Early on in my career, I realized that if I wanted to elevate my "leadership game," I had to continue to learn and grow as a leader. I was determined to become a 360° IMPACT leader. One day, during my quest to understand how I was performing in "my leadership game," I picked up a book. A mind-blowing read that would change my life forever. That book was called *"The 5 Levels of Leadership,"* written by John C. Maxwell. In his book, Maxwell defines the five levels as Position, Permission, Production, People Development, and Pinnacle. The pinnacle, as he defines it, is where leaders have achieved influence and respect beyond their organization. At this stage, he explains that leaders have a lasting impact on the lives of those they lead and serve as role models for future generations.

If you can visualize the results of an atomic bomb going off, that was my brain! A massive explosion happened in the last chapter. I confirmed that there was more to leadership than just a title. This book broke it down so clearly for me that I wanted to learn more (I invite you to read it).

Today, after years of research, hands-on experiences, extensive studying, thousands of books read, and countless trials and tribulations, I have compiled in this book a summary of everything I have learned. And I want to share it with you.

This is a guide to live, lead, and serve in a more colorful world!

What to expect:

Besides a great deal of passion for the topic of connecting to create a 360° IMPACT, this book is your easy guide to impactful leadership. It was written with you in mind! A human who aims to make a difference in the world, by refining their communication abilities, cultivating deeper connections, leading more fulfilling lives, and making a 360° IMPACT in the lives of others.

It is designed to be valuable regardless of where you are in your journey, whether you are a seasoned senior leader or simply beginning your path. If you want to grow, if you want to learn to create deeper connections and do good for your community. If you are ready to become a 360° IMPACT leader, this book is for you!

Each chapter is a collection of wisdom and inspiration, packed with insights and case studies that resonate deeply with the human spirit.

This book is a heartfelt invitation to embrace six fundamental topics—**growth**, **gratitude**, **purpose**, **connection**, **integration** ("balance"), and **collaboration**—as pillars of transformational leadership and impactful living.

It is a journey of self-discovery and empowerment, with the objective of inspiring you to cultivate resilience, foster meaningful connections, and leave a lasting legacy of positive change.

I chose to dive into these six topics because I believe they can move the "impact" edge further. Each chapter is designed to offer practical value in personal and professional contexts. Here's a breakdown:

1. **Personal Application**: Each chapter includes three subtopics that are relevant to personal development. These sections are not only informative but also interactive, as they include thought-provoking questions intended for self-assessment. This setup allows you to reflect on and apply the material directly to your own life.

2. **Professional Application**: Following the personal development section, each chapter concludes a specific segment dedicated to the workplace. This section covers four subtopics that are particularly relevant to professional settings. It's designed to help you integrate the concepts learned into your work environment.

This is intended to be an easy read, a manual you can reference by topic as needed in the future.

Now, there is always a "friendly" disclaimer. As you embark on this read, the thought of making drastic changes in the way you think may be uncomfortable and even a little *(or a lot)* scary. I want you to rest safely in the thought that change is the absolute catalyst for growth.

Each topic in this book will provide you with a simple yet comprehensive framework for your personal development. I hope this book propels you to confidently decide to get off that hamster wheel you are caught in and start living a fuller life, where connecting with other humans becomes a fun adventure with epic results.

I promise to inspire you in your journey toward personal mastery. And your promise to me must be that once you have collected all the nuggets of wisdom I share here, you turn around and do the same for others.

Whether you are an introvert, an extrovert, or somewhere in between, developing the ability to genuinely connect with others can unlock doors to opportunities you never imagined.

Once you let me in, I will dive into a transformative discussion with your brain! I invite you to jump on my "360° IMPACT" rollercoaster and buckle up, because a great ride is ahead of us!

Welcome, and enjoy!

Michele
A quiet and humble Ninja Warrior of my own life.

CHAPTER 1

GROWTH
Fundamental Rules for 360° IMPACT

Be the change!

You are here because you want to make a 360° IMPACT in your life, the lives of those you lead, and the community you serve. You want to live in a better world and know that future generations will have the same opportunity.

At this point, I would ask you to close your eyes, but then you will not be able to read *(unless this is in an audible version of this book)*. So, make every effort to silence all external distractions and do your best to follow my lead...

Picture the fire that ignites within you when you envision making a 360° IMPACT, not just a step forward, but a complete revolution in your life, the lives of those you lead, and the community you serve.

This is not merely about making progress; it is about profound transformation. It is about reaching every corner of your existence and leaving an indelible mark that resonates for generations to come.

Picture yourself standing at the epicenter of change, driven by an insatiable desire to sculpt a better reality. Feel the weight of responsibility mingled with boundless hope, the conviction that each action you take ripples outward, touching lives and shaping destinies.

This is not passive participation, but the relentless pursuit of excellence and empathy.

Picture a life where every decision and endeavor is a testament to your commitment to a brighter tomorrow. To a more connected world, a more human world. Picture yourself leading with purpose and passion, inspiring others to join this noble quest. There is an urgency and enthusiasm to your mission, a deep-rooted belief that you owe it to yourself and future generations to leave behind a sustained and thriving world.

Feel the emotional charge of knowing your efforts today lay the groundwork for a more equitable and enlightened tomorrow. Beyond personal gain, striving for collective advancement, a shared journey towards a horizon bursting with promise.

As you tread this path, hear your impact echoing through time, a legacy of empowerment, innovation, and compassion. See the torch you carry passed on to others, sparking new flames of aspiration and resilience.

Capture this moment. THIS is the essence of making a 360° IMPACT!

A symphony of determination, empathy, and unwavering commitment to forging a world where potential knows no bounds.

With this chapter, I hope to inspire you to let this vision propel you forward, fueling your every action with the intensity of a purpose-driven life. I hope to inspire you to embrace the challenges, relish the triumphs, and hold steadfast to the belief that together, we can sculpt a future teeming with possibility. Your journey towards a 360° IMPACT is not just about what you achieve but the profound metamorphosis you catalyze in yourself, your sphere of influence, and the world at large. May your pursuit be fueled by passion, guided by wisdom, and infused with the boundless energy of those who dare to dream not just for themselves but for all humanity.

This is your calling: to live with intention, to lead with compassion, and to leave an indelible mark that resonates through the chronicles of time.

Integrating the elements shared with love and excitement in this book into your daily practices will drive positive change, foster meaningful connections, and create a culture of high performance, impactful leadership, and strong communication where the joy of well-being *is possible!*

Let's dive into the essence of leadership, shall we? Leadership is the art of living a meaningful imprint on the lives of others. Since this is the case, why do we associate leadership with a title? Like John Maxwell, I firmly believe that we all possess the potential to lead because, with every interaction, we have the power to create an impact. Regardless of the role we play in the world. The question then becomes: *What type of leader do you aspire to be?*

Furthermore, what is a 360° IMPACT Leader? To expand on the concept of making a 360° IMPACT on those around you, you must start by looking at how you lead yourself:

- Are you driving change?
- Are you connecting high performance with the pleasant joy of well-being?
- Are you delivering your message through effective communication?
- Are you connecting with people genuinely?
- Are you fostering an environment where the people around you feel seen and valued?

By addressing these areas comprehensively, you can enhance your ability to drive positive change while fostering meaningful connections and creating a high-performance culture around you.

If you are disciplined and willing enough, you can have it all by leaning into the process of learning to make the right choices.

The following deeper insights into each topic provide actionable strategies and best practices for curious people like you who aspire to make a 360° IMPACT.

If you have not yet done so, please switch your mindset now. From the person you think you are right now *(perhaps because your role in this world has yet to be assigned a "title")* to the leader you already are. So, from this point onward, when I refer to a "leader," I am talking about you. When I refer to the "organization," think of your environment. Finally, when I refer to your "team," it is up to you to define who you are leading around you. Deal?

Here is the premise:

You are a human who seeks to connect with people on a higher level!
A human who seeks to leave a positive legacy behind!
A human who is willing to drive positive change!

As we embark on this journey, let's engage in a "dialogue" to expand our horizons together. This "dialogue" is between this book and a pen, paper, and your brain. This collection of insight is the narrative.

Who are you leading today? Start with: "I am leading..."

_____

_____

_____

_____

_____

What represents your organization? (your home, church, school, etc.)

_____

_____

_____

_____

_____

How are you leading them? Start with: "I lead them when..."

_____

_____

_____

_____

_____

Whatever you have been doing so far to become the epic leader that you already are will be amplified once you inject all the practices proposed in this book. Are you ready to cultivate a more profound impact with those you lead?

Buckle up, and let's let the ride begin!

Leadership is evolving. This leadership evolution is about empowering people to thrive. As you envision the future of your family, your work, and your community, you must embrace the thought to impact your environment in a positive way; you Must prioritize trust, purpose, and diversity (from racial differences to disabilities and neurodiversity). This is essential. To shape a future where everyone can contribute their unique talents and perspectives, you must challenge traditional leadership paradigms and embrace innovative approaches that cultivate a more equitable and empowering world, community, workplace, and home.

The insights in this chapter will guide you in fostering sustainable change. These insights will enhance your approach to a life of meaningful leadership and empower you to make a positive and lasting impact. Personal growth is the heartbeat of a vibrant, meaningful life, propelling us toward the boundless horizons of our potential. It's through relentless self-improvement that we uncover hidden strengths, conquer our fears, and turn obstacles into stepping stones. By passionately investing in our growth, we ignite a spark that not only transforms our own lives but also inspires and elevates those around us. This exhilarating journey of self-discovery and expansion teaches us to cherish the present, make peace with the past, and boldly embrace the future with unshakeable confidence and purpose.

Becoming a 360° IMPACT leader is about working on yourself to achieve growth and success and then helping others achieve their growth and success.

It is a holistic commitment to personal growth and empowering those around you.

Change is the absolute catalyst for growth. And growth starts with you!

PERSONAL APPLICATION

Developing willpower, conquering imposter syndrome, and nurturing emotional intelligence are vital for personal growth and fulfillment. Willpower fuels our ability to persevere through adversity and pursue our dreams with unwavering determination, empowering us to achieve even our loftiest aspirations. Overcoming imposter syndrome is deeply transformative, as it liberates us from self-doubt and allows us to embrace our unique talents and contributions with genuine confidence and pride. Emotional intelligence, rooted in empathy and self-awareness, not only enriches our relationships but also deepens our understanding of ourselves, fostering profound personal growth and resilience. These elements are not just skills; they are pillars of strength that fuel our passions and drive us toward becoming the best versions of ourselves.

Will Power. What is the power of will? Will outshines intelligence or IQ* when it comes to long-term success any day! And I state this with conviction. In a world that often equates success with raw intelligence, there is a silent, steadfast force that is turning the tide: willpower.

[*An intelligence quotient is a total score derived from a set of standardized tests or subtests designed to assess human intelligence.]

While a high IQ can open doors, it is willpower that leads us through them. It is the grit and determination that empowers us to stick to our plans and surpass our limitations. Willpower is the unsung hero of long-lasting achievement. Why is willpower so pivotal? It is simple. You can possess the most spectacular intellectual capacities, but without the willpower to harness them effectively, they remain untapped potential. We might have a high IQ but no interest in filling our brains with useful knowledge.

A few years ago, I made a commitment to prioritize my physical health and fitness. At the time, I was traveling for work every single week and only spent a few days at home in between travels. If you are one who travels a lot, you know this lifestyle includes a lack of exercise and is coated with unhealthy eating habits (unless you are very intentional about it, which is where this story is going). I knew that adopting a healthier lifestyle would require discipline and determination.

I began by setting specific goals, such as exercising regularly and making better food choices. Initially, breaking old habits and establishing new routines was challenging. There were moments when I felt tempted to revert to my old ways, especially during stressful periods. However, I tapped into my willpower to stay focused on my objectives. I developed strategies to overcome obstacles, such as scheduling workouts consistently and paying attention to the ingredients in every menu to request combinations that worked for me. Note: here is a hospitality hack; the kitchen can make anything for you if you see the ingredients on the menu (and face your request with a positive attitude towards your server).

Each day, I reminded myself of the long-term benefits of my choices—increased energy, improved mood, and overall well-being. As I persisted with these efforts, I started noticing positive changes. My fitness level improved, and I felt more confident and empowered. Over time, these routines became healthy habits ingrained in my lifestyle, even when I traveled, and my willpower strengthened.

The impact of this transformation extended beyond physical health. Strengthening my willpower in one area of my life spilled over into others. I became more disciplined in managing my time and pursuing personal goals. I approached challenges with a newfound sense of resilience and determination. Ultimately, my journey with willpower taught me the importance of perseverance and self-control in achieving personal growth. By harnessing the strength of my will, I was able to break through limitations, cultivate healthier habits, and pave the way for continuous self-improvement. This experience reaffirmed that willpower is not just a trait but a skill that can be developed and leveraged to navigate life's obstacles and pursue meaningful goals.

Furthermore, willpower is the relentless engine that drives us toward our goals, helping us to resist the seductive pull of instant gratification in favor of lasting fulfillment. It is the disciplined choice to wake up early, to work late, to say "no" to distractions, and "yes" to focused, sustained effort in any situation or in any area of life.

In our quest for personal and professional growth, determination is the catalyst for transformation. It is what compels us to rise after failure, learn from our mistakes, and persist when the going gets tough.

The stories of the most influential leaders and innovators are testimonies to the triumph of will over circumstance.

Let's do a quick self-inspection:

How has your willpower paved the way for success?

_____

_____

_____

_____

_____

As you look back at your life, can you observe moments where willpower won over sheer intellect?

_____

_____

_____

_____

_____

Do you believe willpower is the secret to unlocking our full potential? Why?

_____

_____

_____

_____

_____

Can individuals cultivate stronger willpower, or is it an inborn trait?

_____

_____

_____

_____

_____

This could result in an intriguing discussion!

I invite you to honor the power of persistence and encourage a mindset shift that values determination as much as intelligence!

Imposter Syndrome. This is a psychological pattern where individuals doubt their accomplishments and have a persistent, often internalized fear of being exposed as a "fraud" despite external evidence of their competence. Those experiencing imposter syndrome may believe that they do not deserve success or accolades and may attribute their accomplishments to luck or interpret them as a result of deceiving others into thinking they are more intelligent or competent than they believe themselves to be.

This syndrome is not uncommon and can affect anyone regardless of their social status, work background, skill level, or degree of expertise. It is particularly prevalent among high achievers and is often found in academic and professional environments. People suffering from imposter syndrome may also experience significant stress, anxiety, and, in some cases, depression as they struggle with their achievements and fear being "unmasked." In fact, with my work as a leadership & performance coach, the #1 challenge most of my clients faced in 2023, the common denominator, was... (drumroll please) imposter syndrome! Some of the strategies I use to help them manage imposter syndrome include talking about their feelings and reassessing their internal beliefs about success and failure.

Being a 360° IMPACT leader means you must have confidence in yourself. You must become committed to silence that relentless voice of doubt in your head. Did you know that doubt silenced more dreams than failure ever could? Why are we giving this despicable voice so much power?!

It is not just about being fearless; it is about choosing to confront doubt with the force of an upper-cut and deciding that no matter what comes your way, you either WIN or LEARN.

Adopt a WIN or LEARN mentality by silencing that despicable voice in your head! Through my mission to inspire and foster growth, I have encountered countless stories. Each one is an opportunity to refine my approach to life and leadership. Yet, it is those who have made an impact on me, for better or worse, who have reinforced my self-confidence. In life, we are presented with two profound choices: to clinch victory from the jaws of challenge or to extract wisdom from the heart of adversity. Which one would you prefer?

Embrace every experience as a stepping stone towards excellence. Both wins and setbacks are pages in your life manual. You call the shots! Be a leader of your own life!

How can you turn the stories you have been telling yourself in moments of doubt into a win or a lesson learned?

_____

_____

_____

_____

_____

Emotional Intelligence. How many times have you found yourself extremely upset over a situation that was, in the end, out of your control?

Emotional intelligence (EI), also known as emotional quotient (EQ), is a crucial aspect of human behavior and interpersonal skills. It encompasses the ability to perceive, understand, manage, and regulate emotions effectively, both in oneself and in others. According to the Oxford English Dictionary, emotional intelligence involves being aware of, controlling, and expressing our emotions, as well as handling relationships wisely and empathetically. It goes beyond just being a popular term—it is a crucial skill set that helps us understand and manage our emotions and how we connect with other people.

Simply put, it is about how we react and relate.

People with high EQ are adept at managing their emotions, which not only enhances decision-making but, most importantly, in the context of this book, interpersonal relationships.

For some, emotional intelligence comes naturally; for others, it is a skill that develops over time. Making a 360° IMPACT involves connecting with people, building relationships, and offering perspective during challenging times. So, if EQ affects how we manage our reactions, and 360° IMPACT is about connecting and understanding different viewpoints, you can see why developing this skill is vital.

This is just a brief version of a topic that is rich and should be explored in depth.

Emotional intelligence helps us navigate conflict gracefully, and conflict is inevitable. Coming from the hospitality industry, I cannot stress how important EQ is because we deal with different people daily. We are in a people-centric industry, each with unique personalities, ages, backgrounds, and the common notion that the customer is always right—a notion we have helped create, I am afraid. However, this "monster" can be managed better if we continue to teach communication, conflict resolution, and finding common ground.

Let's get back to the topic. Have you ever calmed someone down by listening, offering perspective, or sharing similar experiences? If so, you have applied an essential impact skill—emotional intelligence.

Now, let's discuss the benefits. 360° IMPACT leaders use EQ to communicate, make decisions, and understand others better. Why? Because EQ helps us manage emotions effectively and navigate challenges with skill. Emotional intelligence allows us to recognize emotions, understand how they impact others, negotiate effectively, and even influence others' emotions, leading to more successful outcomes in difficult-to-manage situations.

At its core, emotional intelligence involves four key components:

- Self-awareness
- Self-regulation
- Social awareness
- Relationship management

Self-awareness involves recognizing and understanding one's own emotions, including one's triggers, strengths, and limitations. Self-aware individuals are in tune with their feelings and can accurately assess their impact on thoughts and behavior.

Imagine you are feeling overwhelmed and stressed out during a busy week at work. You notice that you are becoming irritable and short-tempered with your family members at home. Instead of letting these emotions escalate, you take a step back to reflect on your behavior. You recognize that your stress from work is affecting your interactions with loved ones. This self-awareness prompts you to pause and acknowledge your feelings without judgment. You realize the importance of addressing your emotions before they negatively impact your relationships. In response to this realization, you decide to practice self-care by taking a short break to recharge and relax. You engage in activities that help you unwind, such as going for a walk, listening to calming music, or practicing meditation. As a result of this self-awareness and intentional action, you are able to regain a sense of balance and perspective. You return to your family with a calmer demeanor and a more positive attitude, fostering a healthier environment at home.

A great way to check yourself is by asking yourself: "Did this situation merit my reaction?"

Self-regulation includes the ability to manage and control one's emotions appropriately. This means being able to adapt to changing circumstances, control impulses, and maintain composure even under stress. Self-regulation also involves being conscientious and adaptable.

Imagine you are having a discussion with a close friend about a sensitive topic. During the conversation, your friend says something that triggers a strong emotional response in you. Instead of reacting impulsively or defensively, you take a moment to pause and collect your thoughts. You recognize the importance of self-regulation in maintaining a healthy dialogue, so you take a deep breath to calm yourself before responding. Despite feeling hurt or upset, you choose to respond calmly and respectfully, acknowledging your friend's perspective without letting your emotions take over. By practicing self-regulation, you are able to navigate the conversation more effectively, showing empathy toward your friend's feelings while also expressing your own thoughts and emotions in a constructive manner. After the conversation, you reflect on your response and use the experience to deepen your understanding of both you and your friend.

A great way to check yourself is by asking yourself: "What do I need to do or think in order to get out of my own head and replace this feeling before I react?" The key word here is "replace" and not suppress. You must feel the feelings.

Social awareness extends to understanding the emotions and perspectives of others. Empathetic individuals can accurately perceive the feelings of others, show sensitivity to their needs, and demonstrate a genuine interest in their well-being. This skill is essential for building strong interpersonal relationships.

Imagine you are at a family gathering and notice your cousin seems uncomfortable and withdrawn around certain relatives. Instead of ignoring this, you approach your cousin privately to ask how they are feeling. By listening empathetically, you discover they are upset about ongoing family tensions. With this insight, you navigate the gathering more sensitively, diffusing tense moments and steering conversations toward positive topics to make your cousin feel more at ease.

Relationship management includes the ability to navigate social interactions and build healthy relationships. This involves communicating clearly, resolving conflicts constructively, and working collaboratively with others.

Imagine that you and your spouse have been disagreeing frequently over household responsibilities. Tensions are rising, and both of you are feeling frustrated. Instead of allowing the conflict to escalate further, you decide to approach the situation with emotional intelligence. To promote relationship management, you initiate a calm and respectful discussion with your spouse. You use "I" statements to express how you feel and actively listen to their side without interrupting. Together, you brainstorm potential solutions and compromise on a fair division of responsibilities. After resolving the issue, you make an effort to show appreciation for your spouse's efforts and reinforce the importance of open communication and collaboration in maintaining a harmonious household.

Research continuously indicates that people with high EQ excel in teamwork, leadership, and negotiation.

As emotional intelligence can have profound benefits in various aspects of your life, I invite you to learn more about this skill. You will feel better equipped to handle stress, make thoughtful decisions, and maintain positive relationships. Once you master it, you will be more resilient in the face of challenges and will inspire trust and confidence in others.

In the magical book of life, every chapter has a lesson we can grow from. Start leading your life with determination, believe in yourself, and pay attention to emotions.

PROFESSIONAL APPLICATION

A leader's influence should radiate in all directions. The adage "knowledge is power" has never been more apt. Continuous learning is the cornerstone of self-improvement for leaders. It involves an ongoing commitment to acquiring new skills, perspectives, and insights. This commitment not only keeps leaders informed and relevant but also fosters a growth mindset that permeates the entire organization. By staying ahead of the curve through learning, leaders demonstrate agility and foresight, positioning themselves as catalysts for innovation and change.

Now, a 360° IMPACT means that when we grow ourselves, we help others around us grow as well. Why is it important to foster a culture of mutual growth? In the years I have been coaching leaders for success, I have collected a series of ground rules that are essential to the leadership journey.

The greatest success you will know is helping others succeed and grow!

To foster a culture of mutual growth, mentoring, networking, peer empowerment, and boosting others confidence are indispensable.

Mentorship. A cornerstone of people empowerment. Great leaders serve as mentors, guiding people and fostering an environment that encourages development and innovation. Mentorship goes beyond traditional hierarchical relationships; it is about cultivating a culture where everyone is both a mentor and a mentee. By sharing experiences, insights, and expertise, 360° IMPACT leaders empower their peers to reach their full potential and contribute meaningfully to the organization's success. This is how great leaders actively guide their teams to success and growth. The role of a mentor goes beyond simply imparting knowledge; it involves cultivating meaningful relationships, empowering individuals, and nurturing a culture of continuous learning and growth.

Let's explore the significance of mentorship in leadership and how it drives innovation and success within organizations.

At its core, mentorship is about leveraging experience and wisdom to support others in their personal and professional journeys. 360° IMPACT leaders recognize the importance of investing in their teams' development, not only for the benefit of individuals but also for the collective success of the organization. Mentorship encompasses coaching, providing feedback, offering guidance, serving as a role model for aspiring leaders, and connecting professionals who may benefit from each other. It fosters a sense of belonging and camaraderie within teams, where individuals feel valued and supported in their pursuit of excellence.

Mentorship thrives on the principle of sharing knowledge and expertise. 360° IMPACT mentors are generous with their insights, lessons learned, and best practices, empowering mentees to navigate challenges and seize opportunities. By creating a culture of knowledge sharing, 360° IMPACT mentors contribute to a more collaborative and innovative work environment. Mentees significantly benefit from the wisdom accumulated over years of experience.

One of the primary goals of mentorship is to foster professional advancement. 360° IMPACT mentors provide guidance on career pathways, skills development, and leadership competencies tailored to the individual's goals and aspirations. Through personalized coaching and constructive feedback, mentors help mentees identify strengths, address weaknesses, and capitalize on their potential. This personalized approach enhances job satisfaction, performance, and retention, contributing to a more engaged and motivated workforce.

Mentorship plays a pivotal role in fostering innovation within organizations. By encouraging experimentation, risk-taking, and creative thinking, 360° IMPACT mentors empower mentees to challenge the status quo and explore new ideas. 360° IMPACT mentors create safe spaces for innovation by encouraging curiosity, embracing failure as a learning opportunity, and celebrating experimentation. As a result, mentees develop a mindset conducive to innovation, driving continuous improvement and adaptation in response to evolving market demands.

During my corporate years, I had the opportunity to be a mentor and to create impactful mentorship programs for various organizations. What I have learned is that mentorship is not just a professional relationship; it is a bond built on trust, mutual respect, and genuine care. Where more times than not, the mentor-mentee relationship goes beyond the predetermined time. I still find joy in mentoring others and always say: "Once your mentor, always your mentor." These meaningful relationships transcend organizational hierarchies, fostering a sense of community and support. Mentees often become advocates for their mentors, paying forward the invaluable guidance they received. And at a certain point in their own journey, they become a mentor too! This is what catapults leaders into making a 360° IMPACT, when they want to give what was given to them.

To become a 360° IMPACT leader, you must cultivate a culture of mentorship. You must prioritize and institutionalize mentorship programs within your organization. You must encourage mentorship at all levels, fostering a collaborative and inclusive atmosphere where knowledge sharing is valued. Mentorship programs do not need to be complicated! They can be formal or informal, pairing experienced leaders with emerging talent based on shared interests and goals. By embedding mentorship into your organizational fabric, you will nurture a pipeline of future leaders and innovators. I have yet to find an organization that does not love a robust and intentional pipeline of future leaders!

Mentorship is a transformative practice that empowers individuals.

Networking. Just as mentorship involves a deliberate and purposeful investment in relationships to foster growth, so does the act of building a network with intentionality. By strategically connecting with individuals who inspire, challenge, and support you, you can create a web of influence that amplifies your potential and enriches your journey. As previously shared, these intentional connections transcend mere acquaintance; they become catalysts for collaboration, innovation, and collective progress. As you embrace the power of purposeful networking, you will unlock opportunities to learn, share, and contribute within a dynamic ecosystem of like-minded individuals, ultimately shaping your path toward greater fulfillment and a 360° IMPACT.

Why is building and nurturing a diverse network more essential than ever?

360° IMPACT leaders connect with individuals across industries and disciplines to expand their perspectives with an open mind.

We live in an interconnected world, and networking has emerged as a strategic imperative for leaders seeking to expand their perspectives, forge collaborations, and drive modernization. Building and nurturing a diverse network of professional relationships, both within and outside one's industry *(this is key)*, is essential for personal and organizational growth.

When you genuinely invest in your network's success, the benefits often return tenfold. The eventual sale, collaboration, or job opportunity becomes a byproduct of a relationship built on trust and genuine interaction. A relationship is built, keeping growth at the forefront.

To be a 360° IMPACT leader, do not just network; truly connect. Focus on the person behind the LinkedIn profile, the title, or the commitment they have to you or your business, and watch as the magic of real connection transforms your profile landscape. I encourage you to ask yourself how shifting your networking approach can impact your professional life. Start believing in the power of connecting in a human way, especially in the business world, because intentional networking leads to professional growth. So, start connecting to engage, to connect, to create a 360° IMPACT, and to grow!

360° IMPACT networking is more than exchanging business cards or connecting on social media. It is about cultivating authentic relationships based on mutual respect and shared interests. 360° IMPACT networking enables leaders to tap into diverse perspectives, access new opportunities, and stay abreast of industry trends. By expanding your networks, you broaden your horizons and position yourself as a catalyst for improvement and change.

Once upon a time, there was a spirited individual named Sarah who believed in the power of connections. Despite her busy life as a marketing executive, Sarah made it a priority to stay deeply connected with her network of colleagues, friends, and mentors.

Here's a glimpse into how she managed to nurture these relationships. Sarah's day always began with a cup of coffee and her trusted planner. Each morning, she set aside dedicated time to reach out to someone in her network. It could be a quick email checking in on a former colleague's new project or a thoughtful text message to congratulate a friend on a recent achievement. These small gestures kept her connections alive and thriving.

During her lunch breaks, Sarah often attended networking events or webinars related to her industry. Not only did this expand her knowledge, but it also introduced her to new faces. She made a point to exchange business cards and connect with these individuals on

LinkedIn, ensuring she could stay in touch beyond the event.

Sarah was also a firm believer in the power of face-to-face interactions. Despite her hectic schedule, she regularly organized casual meetups with her network. Whether it was grabbing a quick bite or attending industry conferences together, Sarah understood the importance of personal connections in fostering long-lasting professional relationships. To keep things fun and engaging, Sarah occasionally hosted virtual game nights or themed gatherings for her network. These events provided an opportunity for everyone to unwind and bond outside of the usual work conversations.

One of Sarah's favorite strategies was to leverage social media to stay connected. She made it a point to engage with her network's posts, sharing valuable insights or offering words of encouragement. This digital presence not only kept her top of mind but also showcased her genuine interest in the success of her connections.

Above all, Sarah approached networking with authenticity and generosity. She believed in giving before receiving, always looking for ways to support and uplift those in her network. Through her consistent efforts, Sarah built a vast and diverse network of individuals who were more than just professional contacts—they were friends, collaborators, and sources of inspiration.

Sarah was my client. She came to me to explore new ways in which she could get out of her own way and network with intention. She felt she did not belong in public settings, always ending up by herself or clinging to the one person she knew at the event. By staying connected in meaningful ways, in ways that felt authentic to her, Sarah not only created a 360° IMPACT in her life, but she is now thriving in her own skin.

If you are like Sarah, start networking with the end result in mind and reverse engineer the process from there. Where do you want to go, and what does that look and feel like? Then create the steps you need to genuinely connect with people in a way that feels aligned with who you are.

Here is another benefit behind creating a diverse network. It exposes you to a range of viewpoints, experiences, and ideas that spark creativity that can lead to significant change. Sometimes we box ourselves into networking only within our industry. We fail to recognize that networking across industries and disciplines fosters interdisciplinary collaboration, where insights from different fields converge to solve complex problems. By embracing diverse perspectives, you are better equipped to anticipate market shifts, identify emerging trends, and pioneer fresh approaches to different challenges.

Networking is not just about making connections; it is about cultivating meaningful relationships that yield tangible benefits.

360° IMPACT leaders leverage their networks to access resources, gather market intelligence and seek advice from trusted peers. A strong network serves as a support system, providing opportunities for job advancement and potential partnerships.

By nurturing relationships over time, you can build a reservoir of goodwill that can be tapped for mutual gain.

Technology has transformed the networking landscape, making it easier than ever to connect with people around the globe. Social media platforms, professional networking sites, and virtual events have democratized networking, enabling leaders to build relationships beyond geographical boundaries. However, effective networking still hinges on authenticity and meaningful engagement.

You must prioritize quality over quantity, focusing on cultivating genuine connections that add value to both parties.

360° IMPACT leaders approach networking strategically, aligning their efforts with organizational goals and personal values. They identify key stakeholders, thought leaders, and influencers within their ecosystem and proactively seek opportunities to collaborate and co-create. It is about thinking beyond your reach and exploring the connection of your connections and the connections of theirs.

Networking is not a one-time activity; it is an ongoing process of relationship-building and knowledge exchange. If you have not yet, start investing time and effort into nurturing your network, staying curious, and remaining open to new ideas. Attend conferences, get involved with groups, participate in industry forums, and engage in community initiatives to broaden your network and deepen your understanding of diverse perspectives.

Becoming a 360° IMPACT networker will empower you to expand your horizons!

Peer Empowerment. Creating a culture of peer empowerment is not just a strategy; it is a philosophy that recognizes the power of collective success. Peers who prioritize empowering others understand that fostering mutual growth is essential for sustainable success. Peer empowerment lays the foundation for a reciprocal exchange of support and inspiration among equals, fostering mutual growth. As individuals gain confidence and insight through peer interactions, they often find themselves in a position to pay it forward.

It refers to the practice of enabling employees to feel empowered to make decisions, collaborate effectively, and support each other in achieving common goals. Which, in turn, helps everyone grow. When employees feel empowered, they are more likely to collaborate openly with their peers. This leads to stronger teamwork as individuals feel trusted and valued by their colleagues. Peer empowerment encourages a culture where employees can freely share ideas, provide constructive feedback, and work together towards shared objectives.

Leadership plays a critical role in fostering an environment where peers feel empowered. By demonstrating trust in team members' abilities and respecting their contributions, leaders set the tone for a culture of empowerment. When peers see their leaders empowering others, they are more likely to follow suit and empower their colleagues in return. Leaders who encourage peer empowerment focus on developing a shared vision among team members. They facilitate open discussions and encourage diverse perspectives, allowing individuals to contribute ideas and feel valued for their input. This collaborative approach leads to a stronger sense of ownership and commitment towards achieving common goals.

In the many years I have been working with teams, I have witnessed the power of peer empowerment as a facilitator of growth. Empowerment is the act of giving others hope, confidence, and support. It is oxygen for the soul. Everyone does better when empowered. In your journey to become a 360° IMPACT leader, get into the habit of sharing with your team how you feel about them, with words and through your actions. Let them know that they are capable and that you are happy that they are there with you. Inspire them to keep going and to make the changes they were created to make. Thank them for their input and hard work.

Empowerment increases self-confidence, determination, achievement, self-motivation, and validation.

Confidence. Lack of confidence, a sign of imposter syndrome, is a common experience for humans, particularly when we are going through transitions and trying new things. If you feel it, trust me, your team does too. The pressure to achieve and succeed, combined with an impression of unpreparedness, can trigger feelings of inadequacy in new roles and settings. In most cases, it has nothing to do with lack of experience and a lot to do with possessing a brain wired to achieve great things.

As mentioned before, imposter syndrome is more common than you might think. In fact, about 70% of people have felt like an imposter at some point in their professional lives. And this is just based on those who actually reported it because most people do not even want to publicly recognize it, which in turn makes it a taboo. Originally thought to only affect high-achieving women, experts now know that both men and women in many lines of work can experience it. Thanks to the groundbreaking work of psychologists Suzanne Imes and Pauline Rose Clance in 1978, we now have a better understanding of this phenomenon.

There are all kinds of strategies, ways of thinking, patterns of behavior, and practical tips for improving the way someone feels about themselves. However, these are all redundant if the foundation is not there. Without a 360° IMPACT leader to inspire their people to feel confident about themselves, lack of confidence becomes a colossal burden.

A long time ago, the President of an organization I was involved with called in a mandatory meeting with less than 24 hours notice. Which was a very aggressive deadline to rally all the leaders who were subject to attending within the region.

He was known as an expert in putting people down. An expert arrogant who loved intimidation. This move was a classic. Drop everything you are doing; it's showtime!

In that meeting, he decided to push a little too far. He told us how ashamed he was, how our parents should be ashamed, and how we would never be like him. He reminded us of the many cars, horses, and cattle he owned. The many properties and money he had. What a bunch of losers we were and how WE WOULD NEVER BECOME ANYONE. As you can imagine, at that point, we could all see our mist of confidence slowly dissipate like a breath on a cold winter night.

After leaving that meeting while holding in tears of frustration, we all had to put on our "happy faces" and "hit the floor" to ensure every guest at the hotel had "the most memorable experience." Not only did he not realize that you simply do not speak to ANYONE that way, but he also failed to recognize that he was addressing the most revenue-generating region with the most profitability and the best projection for growth out of the entire company. My Team was used to producing outstanding results under pressure and with limited resources. How did we do it? We had confidence in the power that *"teamwork makes the dream work"* has.

To make a long story short, as the empathetic Momma-Bear leader that I am, I knew that I had to boost my team's confidence after such provocation. I ended that evening in the office, having everyone write on a piece of paper how these comments made them feel. I invited them to read the story they were "now" telling themselves out loud. This felt not only empowering to them but also helped them regain the confidence they needed to continue to produce the results expected of them. At the end of the exercise, each ran their paper through a commercial shredder. Literally!

The day after, once the dust had settled, I asked each of them to write down a list of the things that made them great. Recognizing and acknowledging their strengths allowed them to reclaim the power they deserved. It allowed them to recreate the foundation of understanding who they really were.

To be a 360° IMPACT leader, you must be passionate about helping people know their real selves. To help them know who they are deep down. To know their values. The trick is that it is sometimes hard to talk or write about oneself, so you must be the promoter of this practice.

Personal values are a big passion of mine, and I often get carried away when I talk about them. I make no apology for that, though – they are one of the most important things you can learn about yourself and are vital to gaining genuine inner confidence.

You see, our values are ten thousand feet down inside us, right at the very core of who we are, and they are the building blocks and serve as your foundation. Furthermore, a value is something in ourselves, in others, or in the world that is most important to us and could include things like beliefs, progress, family, fun, nature, achievement, or freedom.

Why is it that some people and situations leave your team feeling angry, frustrated, demotivated, or deflated? It is because one or more of their values is being denied, suppressed, or repressed. This is a negative experience because it is denying a fundamental piece of who they are. You know those times when your team shows signs of feeling alive, amazing, or buzzing? Those are the times when one or more of their values are being honored, and anyone can get more of that by living according to them.

Your values are all yours, and no matter what happens, no one can ever take them away.

As a 360° IMPACT leader, you must encourage your team to have absolute confidence in their values because they are there all the time, just waiting to be noticed and used. When you get to know your team members' values, you can help them make the right choices and align their work environment with them.

Confidence is a muscle, and like any muscle, you need to exercise it so that it does not shrink and waste away. The problem is that unlike your biceps or glutes, which tend to stay in the same place, your confidence muscle can be harder to find. How do you develop your biceps or firm up your glutes? By doing exercises that are designed to work that muscle over a period of time until you see the results you were looking for.

The same applies to your team's confidence. Let's say that there is someone on your team who does not take many risks, the kind of person who goes through each day doing what needs to be done. And while doing it well, they are not really stretching themself. They might talk themselves out of doing something because it is too scary or because they think to themselves: "I'm not good enough," "I do not have that kind of knowledge," "But I am not a leader," or "I did not really want it anyway." That kind of person lives within what they know and what keeps them safe and comfortable. The fewer risks they take, the less confident they need to be, and so they become less confident.

Become a 360° IMPACT leader by promoting a culture where everyone works their confidence muscle. Prepare them to take risks, big or small. Invite them to be willing to stretch themselves in an unfamiliar direction, to try something new, or to try something in a slightly different way. Help them be open to the possibilities around them and inspire them to increase what they know, what they do, and who they are. The more open they become to calculated risk-taking, unfamiliar opportunities, and the thought of possibility, the more confident they need to be, and so the more confidence they will develop.

Key takeaways: 360° IMPACT growth is characterized by a combination of willpower, confidence, and emotional intelligence.
By creating a culture of mentorship, being intentional in building networks around you, and inspiring peer empowerment and confidence, leaders can inspire their teams to achieve remarkable results.

CHAPTER 2

GRATITUDE
Ingredients for 360° IMPACT

Practice gratitude and enjoy paramount rewards!

The secret fuel for high performance starts with a heartfelt "thank you!". As high achievers, we are always seeking the next strategy to elevate our performance, both in our personal and professional environments. In this chapter, I want to shine a spotlight on a transformative yet often overlooked catalyst: gratitude.

A heartfelt "thank you" is not just a matter of politeness or a mechanical nod to etiquette. Today, I invite you on a captivating journey into the realm of gratitude, a powerful catalyst that could reshape your approach to life as a whole and unlock a new dimension of achievement.

Imagine a world where every gesture of appreciation weaves a stronger fabric of mutual respect and dedication. Envision a home or workplace where gratitude is not just occasional praise but a daily ritual—a philosophy that elevates everyone. This is not fantasy; it is the untapped potential of gratitude in action, a strategy that enriches connections, boosts morale, and dramatically enhances relationships.

Why does such a simple act exercise such incredible power? Because gratitude sees and acknowledges the value in others, it fuels their drive to contribute and excel. It transforms routine tasks into proud accomplishments and turns everyday interactions into lasting bonds.

Think about the most mundane task of washing someone's clothes for them *(I know, I find laundry uneventful, too)*. It is a task that we may complete every day, yet it feels unrewarded most of the time. Why?

Because we do not get a "thank you" in return. How many times did you have to remind your children to say "thank you" after you have cooked them a healthy meal? What about opening the door for someone?

A task followed by a heartfelt "thank you" feels less like a task and more like an accomplishment.

Now, do you practice gratitude? Are you grateful for your health, the experiences you have, and your assets?

A few months back, one morning, as I was getting ready to head out the door, I heard my kids intensely discussing who had clogged the toilet. My immediate thought was: *"Oh great, I have to unclog a toilet now?!"* As I was making my way upstairs with the tools I needed to get "the job done," I realized I was huffing and puffing along the way. It was then that I immediately reframed my thinking and my communication from "**I have to** unclog the toilet" to "**I get to** unclog the toilet." You see, a lot of people in the world still do not have access to a private toilet. In fact, in 2024, the World Health Organization reported that 1.5 billion people do not have sanitation services such as private toilets or latrines.

I could have ruined my day by choosing to focus on the negative, to be upset over the fact that I had to get yet another task completed before leaving the house. However, it was my choice, under my control, to decide to see this from a different lens.

Studies have consistently shown that practicing gratitude is not just a warm fuzzy feeling; it is a power-up for our mental and physical well-being. Because the power of gratitude leads to mindset transformation. Gratitude sharpens our focus by directing attention towards what truly matters.

A focused mind is better equipped to make strategic decisions and capitalize on opportunities for growth.

Here is a list of a few areas where practicing gratitude can create a 360°
IMPACT:

- It nurtures a positive mindset by fostering optimism and joy.
- It leads to improved relationships.
- It helps us build stronger connections.
- It empowers individuals by recognizing their contributions and strengths.

What if I told you that practicing gratitude has the power to enhance your health?

Let's get scientific here for a minute and seriously look at the health benefits of gratitude. The concept of gratitude extends far beyond its emotional and relational benefits; it profoundly influences our physical health and overall well-being. Scientific research has uncovered a myriad of ways in which practicing gratitude can positively impact health, from reducing stress and improving sleep quality to enhancing energy levels and supporting peak performance.

When we practice gratitude, our brains release neurotransmitters such as dopamine and serotonin, which are associated with feelings of happiness and well-being. These neurochemical changes contribute to a cascade of physiological responses that promote overall health and vitality.

Chronic stress can have detrimental effects on health, leading to a range of physical and mental health issues. Gratitude acts as a natural antidote to stress by shifting our focus away from negativity and worry toward positive aspects of life. When we cultivate gratitude, we activate the relaxation response, which reduces cortisol levels and promotes a sense of calm and balance. 360° IMPACT leaders benefit immensely from stress reduction, as it enables them to maintain focus, resilience, and mental clarity amidst demanding challenges.

Want to read more? Gratitude has been linked to improved sleep quality and duration. By acknowledging and appreciating positive experiences throughout the day, individuals may experience fewer intrusive thoughts and worries at bedtime. Gratitude promotes a sense of peace and contentment that translates into better sleep hygiene, leading to more restful and rejuvenating sleep. For 360° IMPACT leaders, quality sleep is a non-negotiable component of peak performance and sustained energy levels.

Gratitude has been shown to enhance immune function and resilience. Positive emotions associated with gratitude stimulate the production of immune-boosting hormones and neurotransmitters, strengthening the body's defenses against illness and infection. 360° IMPACT leaders benefit from robust immune function, as it supports sustained productivity and vitality in the face of demanding schedules and intense workloads.

Furthermore, gratitude contributes to cardiovascular health by reducing inflammation and promoting heart health. Chronic stress and negative emotions can contribute to cardiovascular disease, whereas gratitude exerts cardioprotective effects through its stress-reducing properties. By cultivating gratitude, 360° IMPACT leaders may experience improved blood pressure, heart rate variability, and overall cardiovascular resilience. High achievers prioritize heart health as a foundation for sustained performance and longevity.

In numerous ways, our society has become disconnected from the genuine essence of gratitude. This is quite understandable, as practicing gratitude requires reflection and stillness, qualities that can be challenging to cultivate amidst our hectic and overstimulated daily routines. Consequently, the extensive benefits of gratitude get overlooked.

PERSONAL APPLICATION

Positive Energy. This is when I go from scientific to esoteric; bear with me. Gratitude generates positive energy that aligns with the vibrational frequency of abundance and success. When we express gratitude for our achievements, learnings, and blessings, we emit a signal of positivity into the universe. This positive energy attracts similar frequencies, drawing opportunities, resources, and supportive relationships into our lives. 360° IMPACT leaders leverage gratitude as a catalyst for cultivating positive energy and manifesting their aspirations.

There are so many stories I could share with you related to practicing gratitude and the positive energy it generates around me. However, there is one particularly memorable experience that feels special as it was my "initiation" into the practice of gratitude. In my Junior year in high school, I had a history teacher who was not only an extremely negative person, but she was also very mean. At least, this is how I perceived her at that young age. I loved history, so why was I having so much trouble connecting with her? This lack of connection was not only hindering my ability to enjoy her class but was also weighing on my grades. One day, my mother said: "You need to send her thoughts of gratitude for her desire to teach you." With some reservations at the beginning yet fully committed, I did. I started sending her thoughts of gratitude, and the positive energy she displayed in the classroom was monumentally different from what my classmates and I had experienced until then. I certainly do not know if something changed in her life or if it was indeed this strategy that influenced her behavior; what I do know is that gratitude can move mountains. For starters, this strategic approach pushed me to change my attitude towards her.

Nowadays, I make a conscious effort to practice gratitude regularly. I consciously feel gratitude in every part of me. When I am about to meet with a friend, I consciously feel gratitude for the opportunity to connect with this person. When I drive into my neighborhood, the minute those gates open, I feel immense gratitude for living in such a beautiful place. When I prepare a meal for my family, I make a conscious effort to feel gratitude for being able to use fresh products. Practicing gratitude takes intention and creates positive energy around us.

If you want to make this a habit and need a starting point, here is a tip. Each day, set aside a few minutes to reflect on and write down things you are grateful for. At first, it may be difficult to shift your mindset, but gradually, you will begin to notice a change in your overall outlook. You will find yourself appreciating small moments of joy—a beautiful sunrise, a friendly conversation, or a peaceful walk in nature. By focusing on these positive aspects of your life, your mindset gradually shifts towards one of gratitude rather than dwelling on negativity.

The impact of this practice will become even more evident when you start noticing you are feeling more energized and optimistic. Instead of being consumed by stress or self-criticism, you start approaching challenges with a more positive attitude. This shift in perspective will not only help you navigate difficult times more effectively but also improve your relationships and overall well-being.

Incorporating gratitude into my daily life has taught me to appreciate the good in each day and has significantly contributed to my overall happiness and resilience.

Knowing how you manage your energy is essential for peak performance and sustained productivity. Gratitude serves as a vital component of energy management by promoting positive emotions and reducing mental fatigue. When you practice gratitude, you experience heightened energy levels and mental clarity, enabling you to tackle challenges with enthusiasm and resilience.

Gratitude is closely linked to mental well-being, playing a role in the prevention and management of anxiety and depression. By fostering positive emotions and a sense of purpose, gratitude enhances resilience and emotional balance.

Let's agree that the transformative impact of gratitude on health cannot be overstated. When you intentionally start integrating positive energy and gratitude into your daily life, you will start experiencing reduced stress levels, improved sleep quality, enhanced immune function, cardiovascular resilience, heightened energy levels, and supported mental well-being. For 360° IMPACT leaders committed to holistic wellness and peak performance, cultivating gratitude is a powerful strategy for achieving optimal health and vitality.

Attraction. According to quantum theory, all elements in the universe consist of energy. When someone sets an intention and engages in manifestation techniques to synchronize their energy with universal energy, they can naturally access the blessings of the universe.

I strongly believe that gratitude is a lot more than this. It is to constantly look for solutions. It is expecting good results every step of the way. It involves having a laser focus on making life happier for you and everyone around you. We are not born with "gratitude"; we choose it as a way of living. Choosing to practice gratitude also means that you take control of your life and accept responsibility for your actions and, as a result, its outcomes.

I have a friend who told me not too long ago: *"You always find great parking sports!"* My response to that was that I do because I am convinced I will and all I do is practice gratitude in advance for the awesome parking spot I am about to receive. Using this example as a starting point was a game-changer for me. It is an easy way to give into the power of gratitude and the force behind belief.

The more things you are grateful for,
the better that comes your way.

Gratitude serves as a magnet for more. How does the law of attraction relate to the power of gratitude? It is the law of attraction at play. The concept of the law of attraction suggests that like attracts like. Positive thoughts and feelings attract positive outcomes and experiences. Gratitude, as a fundamental principle of the law of attraction, serves as a powerful magnet for opportunities and success. 360° IMPACT leaders understand the transformative potential of gratitude in shaping their reality and opening doors to new possibilities.

And just so you know, practicing gratitude the day I reframed my thoughts related to "having" to unclog the toilet did not result in me having to clean more toilets. Related to the law of attraction, gratitude and positive thinking have superior power over negative thoughts. Although negative thoughts attract more of the same, the positive energy expelled from gratitude is said to have hundreds of times more power.

Perspective. As in the story I shared at the beginning of this chapter about "getting" to clean the toilet, which brought me perspective, gratitude facilitates a shift in perspective from scarcity to abundance. When you start focusing on what you are grateful for, you adopt a mindset of abundance and possibility. This shift in perspective reframes challenges as opportunities and setbacks as stepping stones toward growth. 360° IMPACT leaders embrace gratitude as a tool for expanding their vision and attracting opportunities aligned with their goals and values.

Success is not solely determined by external circumstances—it is a reflection of internal beliefs and attitudes. Gratitude cultivates a success mindset by reinforcing positive beliefs about one's capabilities and potential.

When you start expressing gratitude for your achievements and strengths, you internalize a sense of worthiness and empowerment.

In brief, gratitude will act as a powerful magnet for more by aligning you with the vibrational frequency of abundance and success. By embracing gratitude as a guiding principle, you will attract opportunities and experiences that align with your highest aspirations and potential.

Now, you might be wondering, how do I practice gratitude for high performance?

Start a Gratitude Journal. Daily reflections of what you are thankful for can ground you and set a positive tone for the day. Express it. Whether it is a family member, friend, colleague, or mentor, never miss an opportunity to express your gratitude. Volunteer. Giving back is a powerful way to experience the joy of being grateful through action. Mindfulness and Reflection. Create moments and make the time to appreciate the journey, the struggles, and the triumphs.

I encourage you to start your day with a moment of gratitude and watch how it transforms your performance. Once it becomes a habit, find moments in your day when you can practice gratitude.

Are you spreading the power of gratitude within your network? If so, how? If not, why?

_____

_____

_____

_____

_____

Start by sharing how grateful you are for those experiences that have impacted your life and career. And when gratitude is hard for you to practice, when you fall into a place of dwelling on all the things that are not working according to your plan, STOP the cycle of dwelling.

You know, a time when the hustle never ceases, and success is a constant pursuit, there is a silent dream-thief among us, dwelling. It is an uninvited guest that lingers far too long, clouding our vision and draining our energy. I am here to remind you that dwelling gets you nowhere. When you're called in its grip, you're not moving forward. You are stuck. Looking back at what could have been, should have been, or would have been. But here's the hard truth: none of that matters if it stops you from acting in the NOW.

I have learned something pivotal in my journey: give these stormy clouds overhead just a few hours to pass. Never allow the dwelling to linger past 24 hours.

That is it. Let the sun breakthrough because like the Queen song states, THE-SHOW-MUST-GO-ON. Transform that energy. Channel it into persistence, into the work that will elevate you, into the dreams that propel you toward the stars. And when your mind is right, do not just hope for change, MAKE IT HAPPEN!

It is not just about dreaming big. It is about ACTING BIG. It is about not letting the pride of the past pull you away from the shores of your future. I challenge you: next time you find yourself dwelling, set the clock. Twenty-four hours, not a minute more. Then, focus, pivot, and advance. Your goals are waiting for you, not in the echoes of yesterday but in the actions of today and the promise of tomorrow. I am keen to invite you to evaluate your strategies for combating the dwelling trap.

How do you stay focused and redirect negative energy into something positive?

_____

_____

_____

_____

Awareness will help you (and, in turn, help those you lead) rise above and reach your zenith!

If you want to be a 360° IMPACT leader, you must cultivate a grateful mindset and watch as the world opens up to you in ways you never imagined.

Now that you have the right mindset, let's discover the ingredients involved in high performance.

PROFESSIONAL APPLICATION

360° IMPACT leaders embrace gratitude. By doing so, they do not just command; they inspire. They do not just manage; they empower. They create an environment where people feel genuinely valued and, in return, give their best selves. But how does one harness this transformative power? What secrets lie in the practice of gratitude that can propel you and your team to new heights of performance? The answers to these questions can revolutionize not only how you lead but also how you live.

Let's dive deeper into this exploration of gratitude and discover practical strategies to integrate this ethos into your leadership style. Try it and learn first-hand how something as simple as a "thank you" can become a profound tool for motivation, fostering an atmosphere of commitment and resilience.

As 360° IMPACT leaders, we have a responsibility to create a ripple effect of positivity in our professional community as much as we do in our personal one.

Prepare to be inspired, enlightened, and moved as we uncover the 360° IMPACT of gratitude in leadership. Let this exploration lead you to a richer, more fulfilling professional life.

Setting goals for high performance can be daunting, especially when your job is to move people to action. Here is the trick: when you have the right mindset, you are capable of setting goals that are both ambitious and achievable. With a mindset of gratitude and abundance, fostering a culture of excellence and continuous improvement becomes second nature. Inspiring and empowering team members to reach their full potential leads to success. Finally, leading by example and demonstrating a commitment to excellence in all endeavors becomes powerful. Once you implement and master this set of skills, you will spice up your journey of becoming a 360° IMPACT leader. Moving your team from "I wish" to "I am grateful for."

Let's dive in.

Goal Setting And Achievement. 360° IMPACT leaders set ambitious yet attainable goals for themselves and their teams. They create a vision of success and develop strategic plans to achieve said vision. They do this successfully because they embrace the concept of: *"I get to"* instead of *"I have to."* 360° IMPACT leaders understand that everyone is replaceable, so they hone into gratitude to tap into the best areas of themselves. They lean into gratitude to see every project as an opportunity to do something greater than themselves <u>through</u> their people.

360° IMPACT Leaders set SMART *(Specific, Measurable, Achievable, Relevant, Time-bound)* goals that challenge their teams while being realistic. All are coming from a place of strength and positivity in the spirit of what is possible. They break down large goals into smaller, actionable steps and regularly review progress. Breaking them down into manageable tasks with clear timelines helps them prioritize goals based on their strategic importance and allocate resources accordingly. Regular reviews and adjustments ensure progress stays on track.

360° IMPACT Leaders understand the importance of setting both short-term goals and long-term ones that align with the organization's mission and vision. They involve team members in the goal-setting process to foster ownership and commitment. Moreover, they provide regular feedback and recognize progress to maintain momentum. When a member of the team falls into a mindset of "I cannot do this," "this will never happen," or my personal favorite, "we have tried that, and it did not work," inject gratitude into the mix and see the ripple effect it causes.

At one point in my career, I was tasked with rebuilding an underperforming operation with a broken culture. This particular project was, by far, one of the most difficult projects I have ever worked on (the details are beyond the point). There were many times when I felt like throwing in the towel, simply giving up. A few months into the project, "high season" hit us like a ton of bricks. Not because we were not aware that this was coming but because we were unprepared from a "gratitude" standpoint. You see, when teams do not operate from a place of gratitude, every challenge becomes a major obstacle. The location of this project was almost 2 hours away from my house. That summer, I drove back and forth every single day for 90 days straight. It was my mindset of gratitude that allowed me to continue and move the needle with even stronger intensity. It was my sense of gratitude that allowed me to move people to action like no one had done before. That summer, that resort saw unprecedented customer service scores. Practicing gratitude helped me make the changes that the team so much needed to feel and the results they so much deserved. The objectives were the same as they always had been; the difference was in the way I broke down the goals for each individual contributor and the mindset of gratitude each team member learned to embrace.

The most beautiful part of it all was to see the culture change from a place of constant complaint to a place of gratitude and possibility.

When you aspire to become a 360° IMPACT leader, you must establish a gratitude mindset and, from there, set aspirational yet achievable goals that challenge your team. They can commit to goals because they see the purpose, they understand they are instrumental in the process, and they can envision the results. This way, you inspire them to be grateful for being a part of it all! I strongly believe that when leaders outline the resources needed as well as who will be responsible for what, each individual contributor wants to take the lead and move the needle in the right direction.

Make a choice right now to become a 360° IMPACT leader who cultivates a culture where excellence is not just an aspiration but a fundamental value ingrained in every aspect of the organization. Promote a gratitude mindset where failures are seen as opportunities for learning and improvement rather than deterrents to progress.

Once you have set SMART goals, break them down into smaller, manageable tasks, and set clear timelines for completion, be sure to come up with a plan to make the results in a visual way. This will allow your team to know how close they are to achieving and gives them an opportunity to make adjustments along the way. The bonus is that it keeps them motivated, and they continue to make strides from a place of gratitude. Because they can see the small wins. While keeping a mindset of gratitude, your team embraces a way of thinking and reflecting: *"I get to work on these goals that will create a positive impact."*

Culture Of Excellence. 360° IMPACT leaders foster a culture of excellence within their organizations by promoting gratitude. Where individuals are encouraged to strive for their best and continuous improvement is valued. These leaders cultivate a culture where excellence is not just an expectation but a habit.

To become a 360° IMPACT leader, create a culture of excellence by instilling core values throughout the organization. Keep your team members, customers, suppliers, and investors in mind, and be grateful they are all a piece of the puzzle. Commit to actively promoting a gratitude mindset where mistakes are seen as opportunities for learning and improvement. And keep in mind that permanent feedback mechanisms foster a culture of accountability and continuous improvement. Commit to creating an environment where excellence is THE standard. Start by nurturing a culture of continuous improvement, where team members and leaders alike feel comfortable seeking and sharing feedback and where learning is encouraged at all levels. While cultivating a culture where excellence is not just expected but celebrated, encourage your team to innovate. Empower them to think outside of the box and be creative. Inspire them to be willing and confident to challenge the status quo. Use constructive feedback and be focused on growth because this is what fosters an environment of continuous improvement.

Teach your team it is OK to expect nothing but the best. The best of them and for them! The key is in staying consistent.

When I was leading thousands of employees in the western division of a company I worked for, I invited my team to operate under the motto: *"Nothing but the best for the West."* It was a catchy phrase that led everyone to make the right decisions in every interaction and in front of every task. All from a place of gratitude for the opportunity to make a 360° IMPACT.

We made this part of our culture!

Development. I never start a workshop without highlighting how grateful we need to be for the effort the organization invested in bringing me to inspire my participants to grow. A company who believes in their people's development is a company headed in the right direction. A 360° IMPACT leader empowers their team members by providing them with the necessary resources and support to excel in their roles. They invest in their team's development and encourage a mindset of gratitude and growth. They constantly provide and create (keyword) opportunities for growth. They foster a culture of trust where individuals feel empowered to take initiative and make decisions.

In your commitment to becoming a 360° IMPACT leader, focus on empowering those you lead by delegating authority and encouraging them to find solutions to their inquiries. By offering regular opportunities for professional development, coaching, and mentoring, you will foster growth and the development of your own leadership skills. This is gold! This is how people feel valued and seen. When they know that you are in it to win it as much as they are, when they know that you are grateful that they are part of your team, they become grateful for being part of it too.

When copied on an email, I had the bad habit of responding immediately. Have you ever been here? One day, I came to realize that if I took a step back and gave my team the time and space they needed to reply, I was empowering them to find a viable solution. At the end of the day, they always found a viable solution. It was the intentional thought of being grateful for each of their talents that I was able to move from a place of control to a place of empowerment. I learned that when you empower your team members to have authority (when possible), and you allow them a space for them to have decision-making responsibilities, they magically start to lean in.

So, look for creative ways to create opportunities for skill development and advancement; this will be a catalyst for your team members to bet on personal growth. These creative solutions can be found both inside and outside the organization. Invest in training, mentorship programs, and professional development initiatives to enhance their skills and capabilities.

For those team members who are in a director or above role, get them an executive coach with a holistic approach. You will be surprised by what this process can do for them and in turn, the organization. And if you are a Director and above, consider requesting a coach. Organizations are often eager to invest in your professional development, recognizing that at this level, you require more than standard training. A dedicated coach can provide the personalized guidance and strategic insight needed to elevate your performance to new heights. And... if they say "no", it might be time for you to leap.

Another creative way in which I found it possible to create those opportunities was by sending team leaders to participate in conferences to learn new techniques they could apply with their teams. Or attend trade shows to find better products or solutions for our operation. Because I strongly believe in sponsoring individuals to reach their full potential.

Commit to actively mentoring and grooming future leaders within your organization. We sometimes underestimate the power of fostering a pipeline of talent.

Since we just got real, consider the following. There **will** be times when you will feel like your department or division has become a "training ground." A place your organization turns to when seeking leaders to promote to other departments or divisions. I know I have felt this way many times. It was an attitude of gratitude that helped me see this through a positive lens. After preparing many future leaders who ended up filling a different region's pipeline, I realized I was doing something right. And I quickly shared this with my direct reports so that they could see it through my lens as well. So, keep developing your people! Keep investing! Keep making a difference!

Lead By Example. I don't want you to be late, it is a sign of not knowing how to manage your time. I am never late for that reason, and... because it is a two-way street. 360° IMPACT leaders who embody gratitude lead by example. They demonstrate dedication, resilience, and a commitment to excellence in their actions and decisions AT ALL TIMES. This means even when no one is watching. They resemble the values and behaviors they expect from their team members.

They demonstrate integrity, accountability, and resilience in their actions, inspiring others to follow suit. All from a place of gratitude for the responsibility and trust instilled in them. They feel grateful and proud to represent!

I remember back in 2007, being in charge of leading a team during the takeovers of four different departments at two different resorts. It was July in Sedona, Arizona. If you are familiar with the area, you know that it can get really hot and wet, very wet. After all, it is in the middle of monsoon season. It was exhausting; we did not have many resources available, and we were all very tired. Most of my team of experienced leaders was assigned to one resort while I was leading the team at the second one. The difference between both was not only the size of the property and the skill involved but also the fact that the one property had 90% of the staff already trained and knew the resort like the back of their hand. I was left with a group of well-intended department managers and a team of inexperienced entry-level individuals, who, fortunately for me, were grateful to be there and willing to try their very best. On my end, let's just say that in my attempt to tend to everyone's needs, my running abilities were put to the test. At resorts like that one, golf carts are the go-to mode of transportation. Let's just say we found ourselves in a bit of a golf cart shortage!

Being very aware of the lack of resources and talent, I had to step it up. I had to lead by example. I met with the entire staff on the second morning (after a very tough first day) and addressed them about the Expectation, the clear goal at hand, and the fact that we could achieve it together as long as we remained positive and grateful. I gave them the time and space to share their feedback and reassured them that we could get the job done by using our resources creatively and staying committed to the goal, together! My message was well received. We turned the house by 5:30PM that day*. Hooray!

[*To "turn the house" is a term used in the hospitality industry to describe when the Housekeeping Department has cleaned all the expected rooms and turned them over to the Front Desk for sale. This resort's due time was 5:00PM (we did great for a second day!)]

It was my sense of gratitude that propelled me to lead by example, put a smile on my face every morning thereafter, and do whatever it took to train the team, operate flawlessly, and keep them motivated to achieve the goal.

To be a 360° IMPACT leader, you must choose to lead by example not only in your professional conduct but also in your commitment to your own personal growth. Embody the values and behaviors you wish to see in your team. Be the leader you want them to be. This will inspire your team to follow suit. With this attitude of gratitude, you not only demonstrate resilience and integrity but also the most important piece in the puzzle: accountability. Self-accountability will inspire confidence and trust among your followers.

To become A 360° IMPACT Leader, cultivate an environment where transparency, honesty, and accountability are the norm. And this, my friend, starts with you!

Key takeaways: 360° IMPACT gratitude is characterized by a combination of positive energy, attraction, and perspective. By setting clear goals, fostering a culture of excellence and development, and leading by example, leaders can inspire their teams to achieve remarkable results.

CHAPTER 3

PURPOSE
Impactful Practices

Living with purpose, on purpose!

We lose hope, and the fun in everything dies when we are uninspired, when we are stuck, and cannot see the way out. Life becomes a routine, a thing we do when we do **all** the things. We become foreign to our purpose, forgetting about being human. Have you ever fallen into this trap? In this chapter, my hope is to help you rediscover your presumption of purpose, so that you can believe in the change you want to make.

Let me show you how you can make this idea sustainable.

In a world that sometimes seems clouded by the hustle of immediacy and the clutter of the mundane, there exists a profound, transformative truth—the power of living a purposeful life. To embrace this life is to see beyond the fog of everyday routines, to pierce through the noise, to reach deeper into the fabric of what truly makes us thrive not just as individuals but as interconnected beings in a vibrant tapestry of human experience.

This is not just about making a living; it is about making a life that resonates with purpose, meaning, and profound connection.

Imagine waking each morning with a heart full of purpose, knowing that every action you take is a stitch in the quilt of your legacy. This is a life where moments are not just passed but are cultivated, where each day is lived with intention, and each decision propels you toward a clearer, more vibrant vision of who you are and what you truly value.

In this life, your passions align with your actions, and your goals resonate with the very core of your being, creating a symphony of purpose that guides your path.

This is not just a metaphor. To live with purpose is to see each day as an opportunity to impact the world positively. This does not mean every day must produce monumental achievements. Rather, living with purpose is about aligning your daily actions with your broader values and goals. It is about choosing paths that lead you closer to the life you want to live and the person you aspire to be. This alignment between action and purpose fuels a deeper sense of satisfaction and fulfillment, transforming the mundane into the extraordinary.

A purposeful life is also a call to resilience. It compels us to rise above challenges and setbacks, viewing them not as insurmountable barriers but as stepping stones on the journey to fulfillment. This resilience is nurtured through the connections we have cultivated and the network we have invested in, providing a supportive base that holds us steady against the storms of doubt and adversity. As portrayed in the previous chapter, let us not forget the role of gratitude in a purposeful life.

Gratitude amplifies the beauty of the present moment, enriches our connections, and deepens our impact on the world.

Remember that by embracing gratitude, we focus on abundance rather than lack, which opens our hearts and minds to further possibilities, inspiration, and joy. Which in turn, leads us with purpose!

So, as we consider the contours of a life lived with purpose, let us commit to the noble pursuit of living each day with a deep purpose. Let us challenge ourselves to move beyond the superficial layers of existence and dive into the depths where life's true treasures are found. In doing so, we not only enrich our own lives but also contribute to a better, more vibrant world.

In embracing this journey, you will find that living with purpose is not a solitary quest but a communal voyage. It is a call to action that resonates with the very essence of our being, urging us to seek, strive, and never yield in the quest for meaning and fulfillment. This is the power of a purposeful life!

A power that transcends the individual and becomes a beacon for all those navigating their own paths.

Let this introduction serve as your invitation to step into a life of deeper meaning and connection. An invitation to transform your everyday existence into a vibrant testament to your values and visions.

Remember that every step you take with intention is a step towards a more fulfilling, purposeful existence.

Let us walk this path together, with hearts open and spirits willing, ready to embrace the profound beauty of a life well-lived. Keep in mind that when you do not know what you want, you will end up with what you get! Without a clear purpose, you cannot set personal goals to strive for. This is exactly when you become trapped in a cycle of busyness without purpose.

PERSONAL APPLICATION

Intention. Live with purpose and on purpose. Another impactful leadership practice. To operate with your purpose at the forefront of everything that you do. Discover your "why." In a world that never stops moving, it is easy to get caught up in the daily grind and lose sight of what truly fuels us. Let me reveal a powerful truth: *understanding your purpose is not just motivational fluff; it is a strategic imperative.*

Knowing your purpose, your "why," that thing that moves you to action that inspires you, acts as your compass, guiding you through life's challenges, and inspiring unwavering persistence. Think of your purpose as your North Star. It is about tapping into the core of what drives you to excellence each day. Maybe it is the determination to prove a doubting teacher wrong or the commitment to support your family. It could be the memory of a loved one's encouragement, or the burning desire to transcend past limitations. Each "why" is as unique as a fingerprint, molding your path and your passions.

When you work ravenously for your "why", every obstacle is a setup to pivot. This makes every victory feel deeply personal.

So, answer the following questions:

What ignites the fire within you?

_____

_____

_____

_____

_____

Why do you strive to conquer each day?

_____

_____

_____

_____

_____

Who or what are you doing it all for?

_____

_____

_____

_____

_____

By Anchoring yourself to your personal "why", you fuel your drive with meaning and direction. You are not just working; you are crafting a legacy with purpose. When you start sharing this practice with those you lead you create a 360° IMPACT. Start with understanding what moves you to achieve greatness. Find your "why". Create a purpose driven life for yourself and help others to do the same. Start a conversation of inspiration!

One of my kids (9) is an ice hockey fanatic. This boy gets home from school, rips his bag off his back and goes straight to the courtyard where he has a pretty cool set up to practice. He does not return unless he has "real" practice, or the sun went down.

To give you perspective, the summer he turned six, one night I found him sleeping in his tent with his entire body wrapped around his hockey stick, like if he was holding a teddy bear. This should set the tone of his level of commitment to what makes him so very happy in life.

This year, he set a very aggressive goal for himself: to become part of the AAA team in his club (he plays for the Vegas Jr. Golden Knights). He practiced and practiced, watched videos, attended NHL games to observe the players' every move (he is not the kind that is dancing in hopes of appearing on the jumbotron, but deeply committed to get more hockey data points into his brain). He intentionally used every resource available without ever asking for a penny towards additional coaching, ever!

During a trip to Chicago, while at the airport waiting to board, I asked him: "what is your intention behind going for tryouts?". He looked at me puzzled, so I insisted: "why is it so important for you to make the AAA team?" After a few minutes of silent reflection he told me: "because it is the right step into the direction I want to go" *(insert mind blowing emoji here!)*. May I remind you that he is only nine years old?

And if you have not figured me out yet, I cannot hold back on sharing the data! The likelihood of a child who plays ice hockey from a young age making it to the NHL is quite low, primarily due to the extremely competitive nature of professional sports and the limited number of spots available at the highest levels. While specific statistics can vary year over year, a commonly cited figure from USA Hockey gives a general perspective: of the approximately 100,000 youth hockey players in the United States, only about 300 will eventually make it to the National Hockey League's (NHL) roster. This translates to about 0.3% or 1 in 333 players. In Canada, the odds might be slightly higher due to the country's strong emphasis on hockey and larger per capita participation in the sport. The Canadian Hockey League (CHL), which is the major junior league in Canada and includes the Ontario Hockey League, Western Hockey League, and Quebec Major Junior Hockey League, is a common pathway to the NHL. According to some estimates, approximately 20% of NHL players come from the CHL. However, considering the broader base of all youth players, the percentage who reach the NHL remains low*.

[*It is important to note that these statistics are influenced by many factors, including the level of play (e.g., recreational vs. competitive travel teams), the resources available to the player (such as coaching, training, and financial support), and physical and mental development.

While the dream of making it to the NHL is formidable, the skills and discipline learned through playing hockey can provide valuable life lessons and opportunities, regardless of whether a player turns professional.]

You see, when your intention is strong and your purpose clear, you can achieve anything! My protective instinct could have pushed my brain to feel the void of the potential loss behind not being selected to play in that team. After all, he has a very small frame. The kids around him his age look like giants *(I guess he can thank me for this... sorry buddy!)*. However, I strongly believe that when we have a clear purpose and work intentionally towards it, anything is possible. So, since he started playing (at age 6), I always allowed his imagination to run free of limitations, to have a clear purpose and work with intention.

Afterall, they said Wayne Gretzky was too small and too slow to make it in professional hockey. So Edmonton's Wayne Gretzky proved them wrong 1,000 times*.

[*Gretzky became the fastest and youngest player in NHL history to reach the 1,000-point milestone, recording an assist at 1:41 of the first period Wednesday night against the Los Angeles Kings. He went on to add five more points to power the Oilers to a 7-3 victory.]

In case you were wondering, my son made the team!

Become a 360° IMPACT leader and share your "why" with others and motivate them to pursue their passions with relentless drive. With the purpose of keeping that passion ignited every step of the way, in every project they work on, and with every interaction they have with those around them.

Reflection. I am of the belief that we do not give self-reflection the respect it deserves. Self-reflection involves regularly taking time to consider your life, actions, and desires critically and thoughtfully. This practice helps you develop a deep understanding of who you are, what you value most, and where your strengths lie.

It actually helps you find your purpose. It is reflection that enables you to make choices that are truly aligned with your inner values and personal strengths rather than external expectations or societal pressures. It is a powerful tool for personal growth and self-awareness. Once you start making time to reflect and allow growth to catch up to you, you start exploring your inner experiences, where you can examine your thoughts, feelings, and actions and make informed decisions about your future.

A few years ago, I found myself feeling unfulfilled despite achieving many of the goals I had set for myself. I had a successful career and a stable life, but something was missing. I decided to start a regular practice of self-reflection to understand why I felt this way and to explore what truly mattered to me. I began by setting aside time each week to journal about my experiences, emotions, and aspirations. Through this process, I uncovered deep-seated values and desires that I had been neglecting. I realized that while my career was impressive on paper, it no longer aligned with my passion for "coloring outside the lines" and human connection. As I continued to reflect, I gained clarity on what truly brought me joy and fulfillment.

As we mature, so should our own definition of success.

I recognized that I wanted to pursue a more meaningful path, one that allowed me to contribute positively to others' lives through my work, but a different kind of work. This realization led me to make a career change, shifting towards a field that resonated with my values and aspirations.

Through intentional self-reflection, I developed a deeper understanding of myself and my purpose. This newfound clarity empowered me to make bold decisions and take proactive steps toward a more fulfilling life. Over time, I noticed a transformation in my mindset and approach to challenges. I became more confident and aligned with my authentic self.

Reflecting regularly does not only help me define any new goals I set, but also enables me to stay true to myself amidst external pressures and expectations. It is a journey of self-discovery and growth, allowing me to live a more intentional and meaningful life, one that is in harmony with my core values and passions. Each day and every day!

The practice of self-reflection has been instrumental in guiding me toward personal growth and fulfillment. By regularly examining my thoughts, emotions, and desires, I continue to gain invaluable insights that reshape my life for the better.

Intentional moments of reflection help us understand our own core values, desires, and beliefs. By regularly taking time to consider your motivations and emotional responses, you will gain a clearer sense of who you are and what matters most to you. LIVE! Do not wait for something major to happen to reflect on it, reflect on everything every day.

This enhanced self-awareness can lead to more consistent decisions that align with your true self, resulting in a more authentic and satisfying life.

To make a 360° IMPACT in your life, set aside time —whether daily, weekly, or monthly—to reflect on your experiences, feelings, and responses to various situations. Writing down your thoughts and emotions can clarify your values and motivations and help you track your personal growth over time.

Meaningful Connections. A meaningful life is about living <u>with</u> purpose and <u>on</u> purpose! One of the most apparent purposes of having people around us is to provide social support. This support can be emotional, such as offering empathy and understanding during tough times, or practical, such as helping with tasks or offering advice. Cultivating connections with purpose means intentionally forming and nurturing relationships that align with your values, contribute to your growth, and enhance your life in meaningful ways. This approach to relationships focuses on quality over quantity, ensuring that the connections you foster are enriching and supportive.

Early in my career, I was eager to build a network and expand my professional circle. Initially, I attended numerous industry events and networking functions, aiming to collect business cards and make as many connections as possible. However, I soon realized that this approach lacked depth and meaningful engagement. I simply did not like it... at all! As I reflected on my experiences, I shifted my focus towards building genuine relationships with individuals who shared my values and growth goals. I became more intentional about whom I connected with and sought to cultivate relationships that went beyond mere transactions or surface-level interactions.

One pivotal moment occurred during a conference where I met a fellow professional who was not only knowledgeable in our field but also shared my passion for community engagement and social impact. Instead of just exchanging pleasantries, we engaged in a deep conversation about our respective visions and values. *These conversations are totally my jam!* This initial connection blossomed into a meaningful friendship and professional collaboration.

Through this relationship, I gained invaluable insights and support that shaped my career trajectory. My friend introduced me to like-minded individuals and provided mentorship that was tailored to my personal and professional growth. Together, we collaborated on projects that aligned with our shared values, making a tangible impact in our community. And shine a light on each other when in a dark room.

By prioritizing quality over quantity in my connections, I discovered the power of genuine relationships that contribute to personal and professional fulfillment. These meaningful connections not only offered support during challenging times but also celebrated successes and milestones with authenticity and joy.

Today, I continue to apply this approach in my life, seeking out relationships that enrich my journey and align with my purpose. Cultivating meaningful connections has not only expanded my network but has also deepened my sense of belonging and fulfillment. It has taught me that purposeful relationships are a cornerstone of a meaningful life, providing support, inspiration, and shared experiences that shape who we are and what we strive to achieve.

Whether you are at a social gathering, a networking event, or even in casual settings, be purposeful about whom you choose to engage with. Approach people who seem aligned with your interests and goals. Starting conversations around shared activities or interests can naturally lead to deeper connections. Relationships are two-way streets. Think about how you can add value to others' lives as well. This could be through offering support, sharing knowledge, or simply being a good listener. When you focus on being helpful and kind, you are more likely to attract and maintain meaningful relationships.

To create a 360° IMPACT, you must shift your focus from quantity to quality in relationships. Do this with purpose and on purpose! At this point, it is no longer just about how many connections you have; it is about how meaningful and deep those connections are. I learned this at an early stage in my career, and it has filled my heart and my purpose bucket.

Let's talk about harvesting connections. Here are some questions for you to do a self-assessment. Remember, this is not a numbers game; it is about establishing relationships that are rooted in genuine interest and mutual support.

Are you nurturing your online relationships as you would in a face-to-face interaction?

_____

_____

_____

_____

Have you followed up with a connection recently just to check in or help without any immediate expectation of a return?

_____

_____

_____

_____

_____

By reaching out, checking in, and lending a helping hand, you are planting a seed of goodwill that can grow into long-term partnerships and opportunities. You do it with purpose and on purpose!

Things that I do to help me stay connected with purpose include offering a new mom to watch their kid so that they can have some "me time," sharing an insightful article relevant to someone's topic of concern, congratulating them on a recent accomplishment, checking-in after I have heard of a natural disaster occurring in their region, or offering my expertise to solve a problem they are facing. All because I believe in meaningful connections and I know my purpose. As leadership eminence John C. Maxwell so eloquently states, the law of reciprocity can be extremely powerful.

The relationships to hold onto are the ones with people who will reach out when they do not need anything from you.

PROFESSIONAL APPLICATION

If you want to be a 360° IMPACT Leader, you must build the courage to ignite a chain reaction of purposeful action! Leading with purpose and passion. Creating a compelling vision that resonates with stakeholders. Aligning organizational objectives with societal and environmental impact. Advocating for social responsibility and ethical decision-making. These are all practices that must be part of your strategy in your quest to become a 360° IMPACT leader.

Purpose-driven Leadership. A 360° IMPACT leader aligns their actions with a deeper sense of purpose and vision. They inspire their team by articulating a compelling purpose that resonates with them. Remember the movie Braveheart? When William Wallace (main character – leading an army) addressed his men, he said: *"Aye, fight and you may die. Run, and you'll live for at least a while. And dying in your beds many years from now, would you be willing to trade all the days from this day to that for one chance, just one chance to come back here and tell our enemies that they may take our lives, but they'll never take our freedom!"* (plop, mic drop!)Their collective purpose was to fight for freedom. This purpose was so profound that the possibility of dying seemed minute to them.

A 360° IMPACT leader is driven by a sense of purpose that goes beyond financial success. They articulate a clear and compelling vision that inspires others to action. They define and communicate a clear purpose that resonates with both internal and external stakeholders. They ensure that every decision and every action aligns with the organization's overarching purpose, creating a sense of meaning and direction.

During the COVID-19 shutdown, I was tasked with leading a team to success. The very same day I joined the team, the country shut down. Most businesses stopped operating immediately, and 80% of our staff had to be let go. You can imagine how hard this was. At that point, the executive team had a very clear purpose: to minimize the risk! We were so driven by it, that we did everything in our power to reinvent our services in an effort to minimize the number of layoffs we were facing, to keep a core team of leaders operating in the corporate office and to provide genuine support to anyone we had to let go. We stayed committed to our purpose, and our purpose became our compass!

To be a 360° IMPACT leader, you must articulate a compelling vision that not only inspires but also mobilizes individuals toward a common goal. Be sure to communicate the organization's purpose in a way that resonates with your team, their values, and aspirations. So they can comprehend the magnitude of what they are a part of. Get them engaged in a language they can understand. This will help you foster a sense of belonging and commitment. Be committed to inspiring collective action. Fostering a sense of shared purpose and direction. Motivate individuals to contribute to something greater than themselves. This will bring the team together stronger than ever!

When leaders articulate a compelling purpose that resonates with employees, customers, and stakeholders, they align organizational goals with the broader mission. This is a great way to emphasize the impact and significance of the work being done.

Purpose-driven leaders emphasize the "why" behind actions, inspiring deeper commitment and dedication.

360° IMPACT purpose-driven leadership transcends profit margins and organizational objectives—it is about aligning values with impact, championing sustainability, diversity, and social responsibility. Purpose-driven leaders inspire teams to rally behind a shared mission, driving meaningful change within and beyond their organizations. Let's explore the essence of purpose-driven leadership and how it shapes impactful outcomes.

Take sustainability as an example. It is a core pillar of purpose-driven leadership, encompassing environmental stewardship, ethical practices, and responsible resource management. 360° IMPACT purpose-driven leaders prioritize sustainability initiatives that reduce carbon footprints, promote renewable energy sources and minimize waste. By embedding sustainability into business strategies, leaders contribute to a healthier planet and inspire others to adopt environmentally conscious practices.

What about diversity? 360° IMPACT purpose-driven leaders recognize the intrinsic value of diversity and inclusion, fostering environments where individuals from diverse backgrounds feel valued and empowered. They champion diversity initiatives that go beyond representation, promoting equitable opportunities for all employees. It is by cultivating inclusive cultures, that purpose-driven leaders harness the collective strengths of diverse teams. Driving innovation and fostering a sense of belonging.

Social responsibility is another cornerstone of purpose-driven leadership, encompassing philanthropy, community engagement, and ethical governance. 360° IMPACT purpose-driven leaders leverage their influence to address social issues and contribute to the well-being of communities. They prioritize corporate citizenship, volunteering, and advocacy efforts that make a positive difference in society. And while they may not always have the time, they ensure a member of their family is "representing" in one way or another.

360° IMPACT purpose-driven leadership requires translating values into action.

Effective leaders embed purpose into every aspect of their organizations, from strategic decision-making to day-to-day operations. They hold themselves accountable to high ethical standards and model the behaviors they wish to see in others. Purpose-driven leaders foster cultures of transparency, integrity, and accountability, earning the respect and admiration of their teams and stakeholders.

360° IMPACT purpose-driven leaders measure success not only by financial metrics but also by their impact on people and the planet. They use key performance indicators (KPIs) to track progress toward sustainability goals, diversity targets, and community engagement initiatives. They inspire others to embrace purpose as a driver of business excellence, by quantifying impact and sharing success stories. They continuously seek opportunities to innovate and adapt, driving positive change in an ever-evolving world.

360° IMPACT purpose-driven leadership is about aligning values with impact, championing sustainability, diversity, and social responsibility. Purpose-driven leaders inspire teams to rally behind a shared mission, driving meaningful change and leaving a lasting legacy of purpose and impact.

Let's pause for a moment and put thoughts to paper. This is an opportunity to get a baseline to see where your head is at right now.

What are the qualities you believe define a 360° IMPACT purpose-driven leader in today's world?

_____

_____

_____

_____

_____

How are you contributing to the driving purpose in your organization?

_____

_____

_____

_____

_____

Visionary Thinking. Do not complain about the CEO, (in most cases) they are visionaries. 360° IMPACT leaders possess visionary thinking skills, envisioning a future that is brighter and more inclusive. As their purpose is clear, they are able (key word) to communicate this vision effectively and inspire others to join them in pursuit of common goals. These leaders possess the ability to anticipate future trends and challenges. They are forward-thinking and proactive in their approach to leadership, constantly seeking new opportunities for growth and innovation. They purposefully disrupt the status quo by challenging conventional wisdom. They purposefully encourage creativity and out-of-the-box thinking, fostering a culture where innovation thrives.

A few years back, while some States highly regulated the use of marihuana, others were changing the rules as we know them now. There was a time when some of my clients who operated in remote locations (destination type of resorts) were increasingly being challenged with finding staff for specific entry-level positions within their resorts. These positions did not require the operation of heavy machinery, yet all positions required drug testing for THC. Knowing how heavy this challenge had become and how it was crippling their ability to maintain flawless operations, I decided to challenge the status quo.I proposed the option of excluding THC testing for specific entry-level positions, as it was not required by our client's policy. This would open up a new world of opportunities for hiring managers. We analyzed the risk involved and decided to test this solution. Who knew that so many people used THC!

Soon enough, in these States, this would be legislated, and drug testing for THC would become a thing of the past for candidates who did not operate heavy machinery. What I am seeking to convey is that visionary thinking means you must be a step ahead of the trend. And when your purpose is clear and strong enough, the will becomes the way.

To become a 360° IMPACT leader, purposefully position your organization for success in the long term. Encourage curiosity and exploration, and create an environment where new ideas are welcomed and encouraged. Where new ideas have value and are always explored, be committed to demonstrating a willingness to take calculated (keyword) risks, driving continuous improvement and growth. Discover your purpose, the purpose of those around you, and the organization you represent; this will invite everyone to challenge conventional thinking and will inspire creativity among those you lead.

Social Responsibility. 360° IMPACT leaders with a strong sense of purpose recognize the importance of social responsibility and ethical decision-making. They prioritize the well-being of all stakeholders, including employees, customers, their community, and the environment. They accept that their actions have broader implications for society and the environment. They prioritize corporate social responsibility and seek to make a positive impact on the world around them because they believe in this principle!

Beyond compliance, 360° IMPACT leaders purposefully embed social responsibility into the fabric of their organizations. They are purposefully and actively (keyword) seeking opportunities to make a positive impact on society and the environment, integrating sustainability practices into their core operations. They integrate social responsibility into their organization's DNA, embedding ethical principles and sustainability practices into decision-making processes.

When you lead with purpose and on purpose, you find ways in which you can encourage and drive that social responsibility you possess. In every organization I have impacted within the years I have been working with people, giving back has always been part of my purpose. Some of the most rewarding experiences I have shared with those I lead were when we jointly worked towards creating a better world either through community engagement through philanthropic activities or by creating and implementing policies to lead a greener operation. Fostering an environment with a clear, strong purpose has always been imperative to me as part of creating healthy cultures. One of my teams took it as far as creating a cigarette butt recycling program where guests and team members knew what the impact of the program was in order to make them part of the bigger purpose.

360° IMPACT leaders integrate social responsibility into their business strategy, addressing societal needs while creating value. They engage in philanthropic initiatives, environmental sustainability efforts, and community development projects. They engage in mentoring others in their pursuit to become well-rounded professionals in all aspects of social responsibility.

To become a 360° IMPACT leader, you must feel socially responsible for championing diversity, equity and inclusion in every sense of these words within the organization and society at large.

Authenticity And Transparency. Carl Jung once said: "the privilege of a lifetime is to become who you truly are". 360° IMPACT leaders lead with authenticity, honesty, and transparency, fostering trust and credibility among their followers. Why? Because this is part of leading with purpose. They are open about their values, motivations, and decisions, even in challenging situations.

It is this type of leader who communicates openly with all stakeholders, even when delivering difficult conversations. They understand that trust is built through consistency between words and actions. They foster trust by being transparent about the choices they make and the grander impact. They openly acknowledge mistakes and take responsibility for their actions, building credibility and loyalty among their team.

You see, 360° IMPACT leaders foster a culture of accountability and integrity. They openly acknowledge challenges with the purpose of seeking input from diverse perspectives to inform their choices. Even 360° IMPACT leaders, although they are in-charge, do not always have the right answers, or all the answers. When it comes to social responsibility, seeking input from the team brings a whole new dimension to problem-solving and diversity of thought.

At a point in my career, a group I was working with was in a difficult financial situation. Some tough decisions needed to be made. It was imperative that the information trickled down to the team was authentic and transparent, yet it did not cause turmoil. By delivering the message to the rest of the team about the "much-needed" drastic changes, transparently and authentically, the team was able to understand the purpose and become part of the change. It was made clear that everyone was needed and that each of them had an important and purposeful mission to accomplish. This minimized the resistance and allowed everyone to feel valued and seen as an important part of the process of change.

Let this insight serve as an invitation to start building trust by becoming an authentic communicator and showing transparency. Be honest and open about your values, priorities, and decision-making processes. Actively listen to feedback and seek input from diverse perspectives. This will help you foster a culture of openness and collaboration. Lead with purpose by helping your people feel safe to voice their opinions and concerns, too.

Key takeaways: 360° IMPACT purpose is characterized by a combination of intention, reflection, and meaningful connections. By embodying these practices, 360° IMPACT leaders inspire others, foster innovation, and drive meaningful change within their organizations and communities.

CHAPTER 4

CONNECTION
Strong Communication Strategies

It's not what you say; it's how you say it!

In the intricate dance of human interaction, communication serves as the heartbeat, pulsing through the veins of our shared experiences, defining our connections, and sculpting our understanding of one another and the world around us. From the tender murmurs of a mother to her newborn to the last whispered goodbyes of old age, communication is the thread that weaves the fabric of human life, imbuing it with color, meaning, and complexity. Yet, amid the noise of daily life, the essence of true communication—connecting on a profoundly human level—can sometimes fade into the background.

Imagine a world where every conversation we engage in transcends the mere exchange of information and becomes an opportunity to truly connect, understand, and grow with one another. This is not a distant utopia but a tangible possibility that begins with mastering the art of communication. It is a lifelong journey, a perpetual exploration of depth and nuance that invites us to continually learn, adapt, and refine the way we express ourselves and listen to others.

The villain in this story: the lack of evolution in our communicative abilities.

Ceasing our learning in terms of communication is like splitting the lifeline that connects us to progress and to each other.

Such a pause can leave us stranded on the island of the past, disconnected from the ever-evolving narrative of human experience. A little too poetic?

Consider the following interaction. A woman in her forties sits at a bar while a man in his fifties occupies the seat beside her. They are complete strangers. She is immersed in texting someone, deep in her phone. All of a sudden, she senses the man leaning closer, prompting her to acknowledge his presence. This incites them to start the conversation summarized below:

(I shall attempt to label the steps in baseball terms to impress my friend Jaime)

STRIKE I

- Him (with the confidence of a winner): "My comment".
- Her (she makes eye contact): "Your comment?"
- Him: "Yes, my comment. It doesn't bother you?"
- Her: "What about your comment?"

(At this juncture, the woman perceives that he carries a self-centered attitude, assuming that she should be focusing her attention solely on him—perhaps admiring his appearance, attire, or whatever he imagined warranted women to cater to his demands... this sounded a little too feminist, I know)

STRIKE II

- Him (insisted): "Your glasses."
- Her (puzzled): "What about them?"
- Him: "They don't look good."

(his comment did not go unnoticed)

STRIKEOUT

- Her (growing impatient): "Okay (in slow motion)... I like them (fast motion)."
- Him (insists): "On a pretty girl like you...I don't think they look

good on you. Why would you wear something that does not look good on you?"

- Her (feels the pressure to have to process his comment at the speed of light): "I don't wear them to appeal to others; I wear them because I like them, and that is all there is to it (politely smiles as she believes in "killing" him with kindness)."
- Him: "Well, I don't think you should wear those glasses because you are too pretty."
- Her (thinking, "I'm sorry, didn't we just meet? WAIT! Did he say "pretty", yet calmly responding): "Well, although you cannot appreciate my glasses, I am sure you can appreciate the confidence I have to wear them in public (softly sharing a smile)."
- Him: [both speechless and puzzled, leaves the bar...]

By now, you might be considering he has no filter or has no game (if the intention was to score). But what if he was the type of person who feels more comfortable starting a conversation with a stranger by beginning with a critical or negative remark before expressing something positive? Maybe he sincerely meant well, but his old-fashioned way of talking to a woman ended up causing misunderstandings and offense. Possibly, he really wanted to have a relaxed conversation, and he just did not know how to carry it through (sure, there is also the possibility that he might have left thinking: "what a b1@7ch!").

Now, let's look at her perspective now. This interaction made her feel a little harassed. It challenged her to think this man does not know how to communicate. To contemplate whether this is the right way to connect with a woman in the 21st century, he should get in his "Flintmobile" and head back to his cave. Or that he is mean and that was an unnecessary remark, because she really digs her glasses, and every time she wears them, without fail, a powerhouse woman makes a positive remark. Or maybe she should not even be wearing them at all!!! (I'm gasping for air at this point).

Although all these thoughts and feelings ran through her head and heart, she chose to be kind in her response. She chose words that would lead him to comprehend she was a Woman, not a "girl." That she was *Beautiful*, not "pretty." And that her confidence was more beautiful than her looks. Because *Confidence* is the new "beautiful".

Mastering communication is more than just mastering language; it is about mastering human connection.

It is about looking into the eyes of another and seeing not just your reflection but a shared story waiting to be told. It is about hearing the unspoken words behind spoken ones, feeling the pulse of emotions that words can barely capture, and understanding the profound silences that speak louder than any speech.

This mastery begins with a commitment to genuine curiosity about others' experiences and perspectives. In the interaction just described, the man could have opened with: "I'm curious, where did you get your glasses?" The level of enthusiasm in her response would have indicated how to proceed. As opposed to going straight for the jugular, without curiosity and a desire to open a door for connection.

Let's keep in mind that he did not have to like her glasses, and he also did not have to strike up a conversation with her. It was his choice, giving him the responsibility to be kind and make it a positive interaction.

If your intention is not to have a positive impact on someone, why choose to talk with someone to begin with? This is what separates this person from a 360° IMPACT communicator.

The art of communicating to connect, is nurtured by a willingness to step outside our own frames of reference and to engage with the world from multiple viewpoints. It requires an embrace of vulnerability, allowing ourselves to be seen as we truly are, and inviting others to reveal their authentic selves in return. Such depth of interaction enriches our lives, providing not just understanding but transformation.

In this day in age, screens often replace human touch, and emoticons substitute human emotions, the need for meaningful communication becomes even more crucial. As technology advances, although it offers us an unprecedented array of tools for connection, it also poses unique challenges to the authenticity of our interactions. Here lies the paradox of our era.

While we are more connected than ever before, the depth of that connection is often shallow.

The art of communication today, not only involves words and gestures like it always has. It involves the conscious choice to connect deeply. Because while we are more connected than ever, we have never been more disconnected before.

In bridging the human divide, as discussed in Chapter 1, emotional intelligence plays a pivotal role. It enhances our capacity to perceive, control, and evaluate emotions—both our own and those of others—enriching our interactions and enabling us to respond to situations with empathy and understanding. Emotional intelligence thus becomes a key element in the communicative toolkit, a skill that transforms basic exchanges into profound engagements.

But, how do we improve our skills to connect in a world that values speed over depth, and quantity over quality? It begins with intentionality in every interaction, choosing presence over distraction, empathy over indifference, and depth over the surface. It involves creating spaces where open, honest conversations can flourish—environments where individuals feel safe to express their thoughts and feelings without fear of judgment. And most importantly, with respect!

As we journey through the narrative of mastering communication, we encounter countless stories—stories of connections forged in the echoes of shared understanding, stories of bridges built over the craters of cultural and linguistic divides, and stories of communities strengthened by the bonds of mutual respect and empathy. Each story is a testament to the transformative power of communication when wielded with skill and sensitivity.

This journey is not without its challenges. Misunderstandings are inevitable, and disagreements are part of the human condition. Yet, it is through navigating these difficulties that we grow, both in our ability to communicate and in our capacity for compassion and connection.

Every challenge is an opportunity to refine our skills, to expand our understanding, and to deepen our connections.

Consequently, mastering communication is not merely about acquiring a skill but about embracing a way of being, a commitment to continuous learning and growth that enriches not only our own lives but also the lives of everyone around us. It is a journey that calls us to explore the vast landscapes of human emotion and experience, to connect with others not just as speakers and listeners but as fellow travelers on the path of life.

My desire is that we are able to create a world where every interaction is an opportunity for enrichment, understanding, and growth. This chapter is a journey that promises to transform not just the way you talk, but the way you live, love, and connect.

Mastering communication is a lifelong journey. From the moment we utter our first words, communication anchors us to the world. It is not just about talking; it is about connecting, understanding, and growing. What happens when we halt our efforts to learn new ways to communicate? We risk becoming irrelevant, making mistakes, and unintentionally hurting others.

The truth is that mastery of communication is a never-ending pursuit. Stagnation is NOT an option. To thrive, to lead, to innovate, one must continually hone their skills. This means embracing lifelong learning with open arms. When you make a mistake, adjust your language. When you choose the wrong words, go back and fix them! Seek to learn to communicate more effectively: seek feedback, listen to others speak, dive into courses, webinars, and conferences, and hire a coach. Be voracious with your reading.

Because each step you take is an investment in your most valuable asset, YOU.

Certainly! Here's the corrected version:

Excuses will always be there: "I am too busy," "I never said it like that," "That is your perspective," "I did not mean it that way." But these are barriers we build for ourselves. Tear them down!

In my years of coaching individuals toward success, I can recount numerous stories of clients who prioritized their growth in this area. Who gained invaluable results from their efforts. From a Sales Director who learns to connect with their team, resulting in them reaching 200% to plan. Or a Vice President of Operations who is able to connect with their boss and eloquently articulate their desire to grow, and as a result, opens up a whole new division pushing the limits of the status quo. To a Director of Human Resources who faced the brink of termination due to struggles in motivating their team, their commitment to learning effective connection skills not only saved their job but also led to the formation of a highly successful team. Within one year, this team accomplished more national-level initiatives than the company had ever achieved before.

You do not have to dismiss people, terminate them, or cut them off from your life. You must educate them on the impact their communication has and inspire them to develop this skill. This is 360° IMPACT.

The more you invest in understanding the nuances of human connection, the more you unlock your potential, becoming a force to be reckoned with. After all, knowledge is not just power; it is empowerment, it is influence, it is impact!

How are you intentionally improving your communication skills?

_____

_____

_____

_____

_____

What resources have been game-changers for you?

_____

_____

_____

_____

_____

Share your experiences with others and teach them how certain language, tone, or composition of words can make you feel. Open the door to learning from one another. Clear communication allows you to do this!

As 360° IMPACT Leaders, we must empower each other with the tools that keep us growing, connecting, and creating impact. Never stop learning!

PERSONAL APPLICATION

Effective communication is not just about what we say but also about how we say it and the moments we choose to say nothing at all. Embracing silence can give both parties the space to reflect and absorb the conversation, enhancing understanding and empathy. Finding common ground serves as a bridge, facilitating a deeper connection and easing the flow of dialogue by establishing a shared basis from which to start. Meanwhile, simplicity in communication—using clear, straightforward language—ensures that the message is not lost in complexity, making it more accessible and easier to engage with. Together, these elements—silence, commonality, and simplicity—can significantly refine your communication skills, leading to a more meaningful and effective 360° IMPACT connection.

Power In Silence. 360° IMPACT communicators embrace the power of silence to form effective communication. Everyone is competing to be heard, with noise all around us. In my humble opinion, the art of silence has become the communication superpower of our times. With constant chatter in our physical and digital lives, embracing silence can transform how we interact with others and how we understand the world. Believe it or not, it is a very powerful way to connect with others. Silence is not about absence but presence; it is a canvas where thoughts, ideas, and creativity can paint the masterpiece of effective communication. When we take a step back and allow ourselves to be enveloped by stillness, we become better listeners, more thoughtful speakers, and, ultimately, more impactful leaders. Leaders who can genuinely and intentionally connect with others.

Silence allows us to tune out the noise and focus on what really matters. It opens our minds to hear what others are genuinely saying, not just what we want to hear. It invites us to reflect deeply, leading to considered and strategic action.

Silence allows us to connect with our inner thoughts, giving space to our intuition and creativity.

In our personal and professional lives, silence can be the key to unlocking misunderstandings and opening doors to more meaningful connections. To make a 360° IMPACT, you must challenge the status quo by choosing moments of silence over the urgency to always fill the void.

Challenge yourself to answer the following questions:

How has embracing silence helped you in your career or personal life?

_____

_____

_____

_____

_____

Do you have moments during your day specifically reserved for quiet reflection?

When are those?

_____

_____

_____

_____

_____

There is magic in silence. To make a 360° IMPACT, you must learn from the quiet strength that you possess. Because when you dive into silence, you will discover the answer you have been seeking. Make time to be in silence because silence is not empty, silence is actually filled with the answers you are seeking.

Finding Common Ground. This is a strong tool to create connections through communication. Finding common ground is a fundamental aspect of effective communication, especially in environments where collaboration and consensus are essential. And this leads to farfetched connections.

Listen to understand, not to respond. This involves paying full attention to the speaker, acknowledging their feelings, and confirming understanding before formulating your reply. During discussions, repeat back or paraphrase what you have heard to ensure you understand the other party correctly. This also shows respect for their point of view. Encourage a deeper discussion and elicit more than yes-or-no answers. This can uncover underlying interests and values that may be shared.

Ask questions like "What are your thoughts on...?" or "How do you see us moving forward?"

Attempt to feel and see the situation from the other person's perspective. This helps in understanding their motivations and emotional state. Consider why someone might hold a particular opinion or feel a certain way, and acknowledge those feelings as valid, even if you disagree.

Maintain respect for the other person's opinions and beliefs. Disrespectful language can close off lines of communication. Use polite expressions and avoid dismissive or antagonistic language, even during disagreements. Get familiar with the term "gaslighting".*

[*Merriam-Webster dictionary describes this as the psychological manipulation of a person, usually over an extended period of time, that causes the victim to question the validity of their own thoughts, perception of reality, or memories and typically leads to confusion, loss of confidence and self-esteem, uncertainty of one's emotional or mental stability, and a dependency on the perpetrator.]

Identify core values or goals that both parties share, which can be a foundation for building agreements. Discuss broader goals or values early in conversations to establish a sense of shared purpose, such as both parties' commitment to teamwork, quality outcomes, or fairness. Ensure that both parties understand each other's positions and the discussion's main points. Summarize the conversation's key elements and any agreements reached to confirm mutual understanding.

Recognize that reaching common ground can take time, especially if the issues are complex or emotionally charged. Allow time for reflection between discussions, and suggest taking breaks if the conversation gets too heated. So, be willing to give something up to reach a mutually satisfactory solution. Identify areas where you can be flexible and suggest alternatives that might satisfy both parties' key interests.

Shift the conversation from entrenched positions to underlying interests, which often reveals new areas for agreement. Instead of arguing over specific solutions, discuss why these solutions are important. For example, instead of insisting on a particular work process, explain the benefits you believe that process will bring. Also, keep in mind that nonverbal cues can significantly influence how messages are received and interpreted. Maintain eye contact, adopt an open posture, and nod to show you are engaged and receptive.

Simple Communication. This is a critical strategy for 360° IMPACT communication, particularly because it helps ensure that your message is clear, easily understood, and effectively received. Simplifying communication can lead to improved interactions in both professional and personal settings. Simplified communication reduces the risk of misunderstandings. It is when you use straightforward language and clear, concise sentences, that you leave little room for ambiguity. This is especially important when conveying complex information or instructions.

Simple communication makes your message accessible to a wider audience. When you avoid jargon, overly complex terms, or convoluted explanations, you ensure that people with varying levels of expertise or background knowledge can understand what you are saying. This approach fosters a more collaborative and inclusive environment where everyone feels able to participate and contribute.

A few years ago, I was being onboarded to a project by someone who used three "big" words for every five words. He had the tendency to use long words, especially when short words would do. As English is my second language and I am a bit of a nerd (watch your thoughts, nerds rule the world!), holding a conversation with someone who uses big words is something I cherish. It is the perfect opportunity to learn and expand my vocabulary. Despite this, my colleague's ratio was way too high, in my opinion. Making his message very colorful yet exceptionally difficult to follow.

So, why do people unnecessarily use big words when smaller words work just fine? In the spirit of big words, here is one for you: "sesquipedalia." Each of those long words is referred to as a *sesquipedalia*. These are very long and multisyllabic words. For example, the word *sesquipedalian* is, in fact, *sesquipedalian*. A "sesquipedalian" is someone or something that overuses big words, like a philosophy professor or a chemistry textbook. If someone gives a sesquipedalian speech, people often assume it was smart, even if they do not really know what it is about because they cannot understand the words.

Did I just lose you a little? My point exactly.

Simply put, simple communication increases engagement and improves connection.

I am not implying that you should not enhance your vocabulary. What I mean is that it is important to consider your audience and avoid coming across as overly pretentious or trying too hard to impress. Messages that are easy to comprehend are more likely to hold the recipient's attention.

People often disengage when faced with dense, complicated information that requires excessive effort to decode. Streamlining your communication is essential for clearer, more effective interactions, both personally and professionally. Conveying your message in a straightforward manner saves time. Both the sender and receiver can focus on the message's core rather than sifting through unnecessary verbosity or complexity. This can lead to faster decision-making and productivity as less time is spent on trying to understand the message and more on acting upon it.

Simplicity aids memory. Information that's easy to understand is also easier to remember. Complex ideas broken down into simple, manageable parts are more likely to be retained. Improved recall means that your communication will have a longer-lasting impact, reinforcing your message over time. When communication is straightforward and clear, it builds trust. Others see you as someone who communicates honestly and directly without hiding behind complex terminology or convoluted explanations. This trust is fundamental to building and maintaining strong connections, whether with colleagues, clients, or personal acquaintances.

Being concise in your messaging will help you simplify the way you communicate and become a 360° IMPACT connector. So, try using fewer words to express your ideas. Avoid filler words and get to the point as quickly as you can so you do not lose your audience's interest. Choose words and phrases that are commonly understood rather than industry-specific jargon or technical terms. Organize your thoughts logically. Use bullet points or numbered lists to present information clearly when necessary. Sometimes, a simple graph, chart, or image can convey what words cannot, making a complex or testing topic more digestible.

PROFESSIONAL APPLICATION

Crafting clear and compelling messages that inspire action. Tailoring communication styles to different audiences and contexts. Practicing active listening and soliciting diverse perspectives. Leveraging storytelling as a powerful tool for influence and connection. These are all topics that are critical to you becoming a 360° IMPACT Leader.

If you genuinely seek to connect with people, consider the audience's background and adjust your language and content accordingly.

Keeping communication simple is not about diluting your message but about enhancing its effectiveness.

Clear Messaging. What are they talking about? Have you ever found yourself asking this question? Effective communicators craft clear, concise, and compelling messages that resonate with their audience. They use language that is accessible and inclusive, avoiding ambiguity. By understanding their audience, they can tailor their message accordingly. They use simple, jargon-free language and provide concrete examples to illustrate their points because their desire is to drive the message, not to sound smart or like they know it all.

Going back to my experience during this onboarding process, my colleague also used a lot of acronyms. A common concern I came to discover during my assessment period working with that team. A great challenge new hires were facing was adjusting to learning the many acronyms used daily. Until they did, they would feel like outsiders. This is a big problem when we are trying to connect with people and make them part of our culture. Especially at the beginning of their journey!

To be a 360° IMPACT leader, start conveying your message with clarity, simplicity, and purpose. Use language that is accessible and inclusive (key word). Structure your messages logically, using examples and analogies to ensure your audience comprehends and can relate to the message.

I remember many moons ago, when I was tasked with helping a team in a remote area in the State of Virginia break free from some bad working habits. Such bad habits were hindering their ability to perform at their highest level and achieve the results that were expected from them. I quickly realized that this team's biggest challenge was in the way the policies and procedures were being communicated to them. It was all too complicated, and the message had to be narrowed down to what they could comprehend. The entire team spoke English as a second language and most of them were not well versed at all.

I could see they had great intentions and a strong desire to succeed. For the duration of my time with them, I made it my mission to be able to level with them and craft my messages in a way that they could relate. This was so powerful that their customer service scores skyrocketed in a matter of two weeks. They felt better about themselves, and team member turnover stopped completely. I was able to genuinely connect with each one of them by making the message clear.

To become a 360° IMPACT leader, you can also reinforce your message through multiple channels and repeat it as necessary for comprehension. Communicating expectations clearly helps the team move in the right direction at a faster speed.

Active Listening. "Are you even listening?" Words that have come out of my mouth too many times. 360° IMPACT Leaders practice active listening, seeking to understand other people's perspectives and concerns without judgment. They demonstrate empathy and respect for diverse viewpoints. They ask clarifying questions, paraphrase what they hear, and demonstrate empathy and understanding. Practicing empathic listening means seeking to understand the underlying emotions and motivations behind other people's words. It means demonstrating genuine interest and curiosity, fostering trust and rapport. Listening to understand, and not just to respond. This is especially important when the person speaking with you is in need of empathy and is not necessarily seeking an immediate response from you. This is how you connect!

For years, I traveled across the country, collaborating with teams at various hotels. During these visits, an important representative would occasionally stop by. It was crucial for local leaders to engage with this visitor, yet my observation indicated these interactions were often strained. Their focus was not on establishing rapport or genuinely connecting with the staff.

Observing this was difficult. In these situations, my goal was to ensure that the teams understood the intended messages clearly and did not misinterpret the visitor's level of engagement as a reflection of their own efforts to connect.

Actively listening to people is a skill that can be learned.

To be a 360° IMPACT leader, practice empathy and validation and seek to connect with others on a deeper level, which in turn will build trust through genuine engagement. Ask probing questions, paraphrase key points, and validate feelings to foster meaningful dialogue and connection. Start by listening, then acknowledge their emotions and experiences, and close with paraphrasing key points to ensure mutual understanding and commitment.

It is the practice of active listening that fosters stronger connections, builds trust, and promotes effective collaboration.

Adaptability In Communication. 360° IMPACT Leaders tailor their communication style to suit different audiences and contexts. They recognize the importance of verbal and nonverbal cues in conveying meaning and building rapport with the people they lead. This is, in part, what leads to genuine connections between people.

360° IMPACT leaders adapt their communication style to suit the situation and the preferences of their audience. They are comfortable communicating in person, in writing, and through digital channels. Whether it is by adjusting their tone, language, or medium.

Let's break this down:

- **Tone**: this involves changing the emotional and expressive quality of your voice, which can influence how the message is perceived. For example, you might use a more serious tone when discussing important business matters or a lighter tone for casual conversation.
- **Language**: this means using different vocabulary or structuring sentences differently. It could involve using simpler words for a general audience or more specialized jargon for experts.
- **Medium**: this refers to changing the method of delivery of the message. For instance, they may opt for an email instead of a phone call (or vice versa), a written report instead of a verbal presentation, or social media instead of a formal letter.

When I work with professionals who have difficulty connecting with others through their communication, I often request them to "replay" the conversation for me.

Frequently, I find myself advising my clients that it is time to make a phone call instead. Emails can often be misinterpreted, and persisting with this approach can severely damage the relationship.

Adjusting your approach based on factors such as cultural background, personality types, generation, and preferred channels of communication is critical. This opens a gate to ensure there is effective engagement on the other side.

To be a 360° IMPACT leader, be mindful of cultural nuances and how the message may be received. Keep individual preferences at the forefront. Bear in mind that flexibility in communication enhances understanding and promotes inclusivity.

One last story relates to the use of body language in our communication. Early in my career, while addressing a large group of team members, at some point in the message, I snapped my fingers while referring to speed. Although my intention was to enhance my message for any visual and auditory learners in the room, there was one team member who found my finger snapping incredibly offensive. I am grateful, to this day, that she felt comfortable enough to share this with me. She explained that finger snapping is used for animals in her home country. I was devastated for making her feel like I was not treating her with the respect she deserved. Her approach gave me an opportunity to genuinely connect with her.

Storytelling, Analogies And Numbers. Another impactful way to connect with people is through the use of storytelling and analogies. 360° IMPACT Leaders leverage the power of storytelling and analogies to engage and inspire others. To convey complex ideas, evoke emotions, and motivate action. Helping their audience emotionally connect with the story and better understand complex ideas. Making their message more accessible and memorable. They use vivid imagery, compelling characters, and relatable anecdotes to bring their message to life and create a lasting impression. They focus on conveying key messages through storytelling and analogies.

What about the use of numbers to create a connection? Using numbers to create a connection can be a powerful tool in communication, especially in settings where precision and evidence are valued. Quantitative data can enhance the credibility of your message. Providing statistics, percentages, or specific figures can support your arguments and make them more persuasive. Numbers can clarify the magnitude or importance of what you are discussing. They can help quantify changes, growth, or comparisons, making abstract concepts more concrete and understandable.

Well-presented data can catch and hold the audience's attention, especially when it surprises or challenges their expectations. Graphs, charts, and infographics can visually engage people, making complex information easier to digest. Numbers are often easier to remember than abstract narratives. A compelling statistic or a surprising figure can stick in someone's memory, reinforcing the connection between the speaker and the audience.

Numbers can also evoke an emotional response, particularly when they highlight significant truths, such as the impact of a problem or the effectiveness of a solution. This can strengthen the emotional connection with the audience.

Many organizations effectively use numbers to convey messages, emphasize their impact, or highlight needs. Let's look at some examples from various industries, both in the public and private sectors:

- **World Health Organization**: uses statistics to communicate health-related issues to the public. For instance, they provide numbers on global incidences of diseases, vaccination rates, and health service coverage, which help raise awareness and shape public health policies.

- **World Wildlife Fund**: uses numbers to highlight the urgency of wildlife and habitat conservation. They often share data about species population declines, percentages of forest loss, or the amount of plastic dumped in oceans annually to drive home the importance of conservation efforts.

- **United Nations**: uses data extensively in its reports and communications to discuss progress on the Sustainable Development Goals (SDGs). They provide metrics on poverty levels, access to clean water, education rates, and many other global issues to inform and mobilize international action.

- **NASA**: The U.S. space agency frequently uses data to convey the magnitude of their projects and missions. Whether it's distances between celestial bodies, sizes of planets, or timelines of space exploration, these numbers help the public understand the scope and scale of space science.

- **Apple Inc.**: uses numbers in its product launches and annual reports to highlight sales figures, revenue growth, and user statistics. They often announce the number of iPhones sold in a quarter, app downloads from the App Store, or the growth in Apple Music subscribers to showcase their market success.

- **Tesla, Inc.**: emphasizes numerical data in its communications to demonstrate technological advancements and market leadership in electric vehicles and renewable energy. They share production numbers, vehicle deliveries, energy storage deployments, and battery performance metrics to showcase their innovation and growth.

- **Uber Technologies, Inc.**: uses numbers extensively in its communications to highlight the scale of its operations and the impact on transportation. They share metrics on the number of rides completed, drivers on the platform, cities served, and growth in food delivery services (Uber Eats) to demonstrate their market presence and expansion.

- **Amazon**: Amazon utilizes numbers to convey its dominance in e-commerce and cloud computing. They often report metrics like revenue growth, Prime membership numbers, fulfillment center locations, and AWS (Amazon Web Services) market share to demonstrate their business performance and market position.
- **Marriott International** incorporates numerical data into its communications to highlight its global presence, guest satisfaction, and business performance.

Incorporating numbers into your communication can be an effective way to connect with your audience, lending weight to your messages and making them more impactful and memorable.

What about using numbers and images? Let's take the example of **Corona**. In 2019, the "Plastic Ocean" campaign by Corona, a beer brand, highlighted the issue of plastic pollution in the oceans. The campaign featured a striking visual of thousands of plastic bottles strung together to create a "belt" across the ocean. This impactful image was intended to raise awareness about the detrimental effects of plastic waste on marine life and the environment. The message conveyed through this advertisement was that plastic pollution has become a pervasive and destructive problem, symbolized by the visual representation of a belt made of discarded plastic bottles spanning the ocean. The campaign aimed to encourage consumers to reduce their use of single-use plastics and support initiatives for ocean conservation. Corona's "Plastic Ocean" campaign exemplifies how creative advertising can use powerful visuals and symbolism, including numerical representations (such as the sheer quantity of plastic bottles used), to effectively communicate complex environmental issues and inspire action toward positive change.

In your journey of becoming a 360° IMPACT leader, inject storytelling into the way you deliver your message and watch the magic of connection unfold before your eyes. Use narratives to your advantage to engage, inspire, and motivate your audience. Share stories that resonate emotionally and convey key messages in a memorable and compelling way. When you have to prepare a presentation, use vivid imagery, descriptive language, and relatable characters to bring your message to life. Storytelling creates emotional connections, engages audiences, and drives action.

Key takeaways: 360° IMPACT connection is characterized by a combination of silence, finding common ground, and simplifying communication. 360° IMPACT leaders can build stronger connections, foster trust, and inspire positive change within their teams and communities by incorporating these strategies into their communication practices.

CHAPTER 5

INTEGRATION (a.k.a. balance) Promoting Well-being and Joy

Boundaries can take you far! (sounds crazy, I know!)

We all strive to live a balanced and perfect life. However, we need a little imperfection to judge things and know what is right from wrong. To distinguish between too much or too little. If you have lived it, you can distinguish it. Because it is the things that go wrong in life, that make life so much more valuable.

I believe we need to know what imperfection feels like to know, understand, and seek perfection. It is that pursuit of perfection that puts us in a constant search for growth. We never achieve perfection if we are in constant evolution. And this, my friend, is what makes life so perfect!

Being able to be aware of our emotions, to live those emotions and feel them with every sense, is what allows us to be in such a constant state of growth. And when we adjust our mindset to strongly believe that growth is the ultimate sense of perfection, we can live life to our fullest and embrace all its colors.

To embrace this life is to see beyond the fog of everyday routines, to reach deeper into what truly makes us thrive not just as individuals but as interconnected beings. This is not just about making a living; it is about making a life that resonates with purpose, meaning, and profound connection. A life of *"integration"* instead of *"balance."* Because balance leads us to believe there are only two sides, while life is a combination of everything. And by "everything," I mean health, personal growth, fun, leisure, career, money, friends, family, and home environment.

So instead of seeking balance, how about we start seeking integration? A perfectly imperfect amalgamation of everything that brings us joy, that makes us who we truly are.

I know this sounds like a radical theory, but bear with me. I challenge you to make an effort right now and switch your brain from what you know as "balance" to this new concept of "integration". Stay with me...

Imagine waking each morning with a heart full of *integration*, where every single one of your cups is full. Knowing that every action you take is a stitch in the quilt of your legacy. This is a life where moments are not just passed but are cultivated, where each day is lived with intention, and each decision propels you toward a clearer, more vibrant vision of who you are and what you truly value. The perfectly imperfect composition of all the things that make life so wonderful. In this life, your passions align with your actions, positively impacting every area of your life, and your goals resonate with the very core of your being, creating a symphony of purpose that guides your path.

But how do we cultivate such a life?

It begins with connections, deep, genuine, heartfelt connections. Think of all humans as a colorful piece of fabric. We are all threads, intertwined. Where the strength of our bond enhances the resilience of the whole. To live an integrated life (or balanced life), we must connect with each other, our needs, our wants, and our aspirations. We need to connect on a deeper, higher level.

To cultivate connections is to recognize the profound impact of every relationship in our lives, from fleeting interactions to deep, enduring friendships. It is to approach each connection with kindness, empathy, and a genuine interest in the welfare of others. It is about weaving a community where every member uplifts and supports one another because this is what impacts every aspect of our life, bringing integration or balance to it.

Living an integrated life also means investing in your network's success. Those in your circle are the ones who you can lean on and find that "balance" when needed. This is where the magic of reciprocity breathes life into our ambitions. When you invest in the success of others, you are not just fostering goodwill; you are setting the stage for mutual growth and enrichment. This investment doesn't require grand gestures; often, it is the small acts of encouragement, the sharing of resources, or the Offering of your time and expertise that ignite a chain reaction of positive outcomes. In every aspect of your life!

By championing the successes of those around you, you create an environment ripe for innovation and opportunity for yourself and the collective. This is a connection!

To live with integration is to see each day as an opportunity to positively impact the world. It is about aligning your daily actions with your broader values and goals. It is about choosing paths that lead you closer to the life you want to live and the person you aspire to be. This alignment between action and integration fuels a deeper sense of satisfaction and fulfillment, transforming the mundane into the extraordinary.

Let us not forget the role of gratitude in an integrated life. As I mentioned in Chapter 2, gratitude amplifies the beauty of the present moment, enriches our connections, and deepens our impact on the world. By embracing gratitude, we focus on abundance rather than lack, which opens our hearts and minds to further possibilities, inspiration, and joy—all leading to a fuller, richer, more integrated life.

So, as we consider the contours of a life lived with integration, let us commit to these noble pursuits: cultivating meaningful connections, investing in the collective success of our networks, and living each day with a resonant purpose. Let us challenge ourselves to move beyond the superficial layers of existence and dive into the depths where life's true treasures are found. In doing so, we not only enrich our own lives but also contribute to a better, more vibrant world.

In embracing this journey, you will find that living with purpose is not a solitary quest but a communal voyage. It is a call to action that resonates with the very essence of our being, urging us to seek, strive, and never yield in the pursuit of meaning and fulfillment. This is the power of an integrated life, a power that transcends the individual and becomes a beacon for all those navigating their own paths.

Let this introduction serve as your invitation to step into a life of deeper meaning and connection. An invitation to transform your everyday existence into a vibrant testament to your values and visions. A life with integration. As you step into this chapter, remember that every step taken with intention is a step towards a more fulfilling, purposeful, and integrated existence.

I now invite you to embrace the profound beauty of a life well-lived.

You have tried every productivity hack and downloaded every app that promised a utopia of work-life balance. Yet, the more you chase, the more that perfect harmony evades you. It leaves you feeling drained, stressed out, and hopelessly juggling your commitments. Once again, balance is two-sided, while integration encompasses everything.

You are not alone in this relentless pursuit that feels like running on a hamster wheel.

Imagine missing another of your kid's soccer games because a meeting ran late or scrolling through emails during a family dinner. The guilt creeps in, adding weight to your already heavy shoulders.

What if you were to find the way to integrate it all, to make time and space for everything that brings you joy, that brings joy to your family, your community, and ultimately the world?

You feel stuck in this cycle of constant compromise, believing that if you could just get that balance right, everything would fall into place. But what if the scales are rigged against you? What if the chase is pointless, leaving you less present and more frustrated than ever?

What if I told you that work-life balance doesn't exist? What if I told you that it is actually all about *work-life priorities*? All about integration. It is not about dividing your life into perfect slices of work and play. It is about integrating your responsibilities and passions in a way that feels right to you.

It is time for you to discover how to make more meaningful integrated choices that resonate with your unique situation.

It is time for you to prioritize what truly matters without the constant tug-of-war between office and home.

It is time for you to transform your decision-making process to reduce stress and increase satisfaction for yourself and those you impact around you.

It is time to look at life as a composition and arrangement of all the things that make your life yours.

With this chapter, my intention is for you to gain a new perspective so that you can craft a life where your professional success and personal fulfillment are not at odds but in harmony, according to **your** standards.

I encourage you to say goodbye to the mythical one-size-fits-all balance and hello to a tailored, dynamic lifestyle that adapts to your needs. *An integrated life!*

It is time for you to gain the clarity and confidence to make choices that lead to a genuinely content and integrated life by **your** definition. Creating your personalized path. Take the first step towards a life from which you don't need a vacation. Embrace the change and watch your world transform from black-and-white to vibrant color.

Stop chasing.

Start living!

PERSONAL APPLICATION

In your pursuit of integration, you must embrace the fact that it has everything to do with the choices you make at the time you make them. And for this, it is imperative you start learning to respect yourself, to set healthy boundaries and to be committed to never depleting your reserve tank.

Self-respect. For you to live a 360° IMPACT integrated life you must respect others, and you cannot respect others unless you start by respecting yourself, and embracing who you are.

As we navigate the currents of social expectations, it is easy to forget the power of embracing our true selves. Learning about who you are, what weaknesses and strengths you bring to the table, and finding viable solutions to either get better or embrace them is pivotal to personal growth. You must know your values and purpose in life as described in Chapter 3, to craft a life of integration.

Here is my story of embracing who I am. As an introvert, attending public events can be a tidal wave of stimulation, leaving me gasping for breath in a sea of interactions. But there is a lifebuoy I have learned to cling to: it is entirely okay to take a "time out." Yes, just like we put a child on time out when they are misbehaving, which typically has to do with them being overstimulated or tired (at least this is what I learned through my children).

Sometimes, I pull a ninja move, and I vanish discreetly, granting myself a precious half-hour to recalibrate my energy and recharge my social batteries. It is not an escape; it is self-care, and it is vital.

Being a foreigner adds another layer to the mix. For years, my accent felt like weights tied to my tongue, anchoring down my confidence. And here is the truth I have come to cherish. I may speak with an accent, but I do not think with one.

Why the context? Because I know that you might need to learn to embrace and respect yourself as well. I have learned to be at peace with my uniqueness and to wear my introversion and accent as a badge of my journey. This peace is not just for introverts or for those with accents; it is a universal truth. It is about respecting who you are, with all your quirks and characteristics. So, starting today, I invite you to stand a little taller, demonstrate self-respect, and demand it from the world because at day's end, and in the silence of your own company, you are the one you answer to.

If you want to become a 360° IMPACT leader, you must celebrate your individuality and respect your personal needs.

Take a minute to reflect:

Do you have a unique trait or practice that you have come to embrace?

_____

_____

_____

_____

_____

Create a new narrative where self-acceptance is at the forefront because that is what helps us understand, adjust, and grow. It is imperative that we inspire one another to respect our singular selves. This is what diversity, equity, inclusion, and belonging are all about!

How do you honor and respect your authentic self?

_____

_____

_____

_____

_____

Spread the wave of self-acceptance and respect. If you haven't yet, start embracing your unique self now!

Boundaries. Learning to say "no" is necessary as a step towards self-respect and vice versa. Effective boundary-setting supports healthy communication and fosters wellness, productivity, and self-respect. Saying "no" helps preserve valuable resources like time and energy, enhances performance by focusing on strengths, and promotes clarity in priorities. It also aids in relationship management by establishing clear expectations and reducing stress associated with over-commitment. Learning to say "no" is a key skill that empowers individuals to make intentional choices aligned with their values and goals. This leads to 360° IMPACT integration.

When you recognize that you are enough, you feel stronger about saying: "Enough!"

In both personal and professional contexts, your time is a limited resource. Saying "no" helps you manage your time more effectively, allowing you to prioritize tasks and engagements that align with your goals and responsibilities.

Tasks and commitments require mental, emotional, and physical energy. Saying "no" prevents overcommitment, which can lead to burnout and decreased productivity. By saying "no" to tasks that are outside your skill set or interests, you can focus on what you excel at, enhancing your performance and contribution. Taking on fewer commitments can lead to better outcomes because you can dedicate appropriate time and effort to each task.

Saying "no" is a key part of asserting your personal boundaries, which is essential for mental health and well-being. It communicates to others what you are comfortable with and how you expect to be treated. In work environments (and this includes your work at home), clear boundaries regarding workload and roles can prevent miscommunications and ensure that responsibilities are evenly distributed and understood. Communicating your limits honestly helps build trust in both personal and professional relationships. People tend to respect those who can express their limits clearly and respectfully.

When you say "yes" too often, especially when you do not want to, it can lead to feelings of resentment towards others who may be unknowingly imposing on you. Being able to say "no" is a sign of assertiveness, which is an important communication skill. It shows that you value your own needs and are willing to advocate for yourself. Furthermore, regularly exercising your ability to decline requests can boost your confidence in making decisions that are best for you and not just those around you. This leads to making space for integration. Because every time you say "yes" to something, you are saying "no" to something else due to the limitations of your resources. Saying "no" can free up opportunities to say "yes" to more suitable, beneficial, fulfilling, and integrated alternatives.

Saying "no" helps clarify to yourself and others what your priorities really are. It keeps your objectives clear and aligned with your personal or professional vision.

Not overcommitting reduces the pressure and stress that come with trying to meet too many demands or manage too many tasks at once.

In the turbulence of modern life, where ambitions soar, and demands press upon us from every angle, there exists a serene island of wisdom that too few of us choose to inhabit. It is the gentle philosophy of not overcommitting, a principle that can profoundly reshape your life by stripping away undue pressure and stress. This idea is not about doing less for the sake of laziness but about doing what you can manage with fervor and excellence, where you are able to integrate every aspect of your life. It is about finding joy in your engagements, relishing each task, and giving each commitment the attention it truly deserves.

You must begin by envisioning your daily life not as a frantic race against the clock but as a carefully curated collection of tasks and responsibilities, each chosen with intention and foresight.

Overcommitment is parallel to a juggler adding one too many balls to their act. Initially, it may seem feasible, perhaps even exhilarating, to keep all the balls in the air. But soon, the thrill fades, replaced by the creeping realization that control is slipping away. Balls begin to drop, and the juggler's performance suffers.

When you overcommit, you mirror this juggler. You take on more tasks than you can handle, not because you are capable, but because you fear missing out, or you fear disappointing others, or perhaps because you have not taken the time to truly understand your own limits. You say "yes" when you should say "no," not out of a desire to be helpful but out of a misplaced sense of obligation or a quest for validation that comes from being seen as capable, busy, and indispensable.

The consequences of overcommitment are severe and multifaceted. Stress and pressure mount not just as abstract concepts but as palpable forces that fray your nerves and wear down your spirits. Your health, both mental and physical, begins to falter. Sleep becomes elusive, anxiety creeps in, and your overall well-being declines. Relationships suffer, too, as you have less quality time to offer, and when you are present, your exhausted mind detracts from your ability to be truly there.

What if you chose another path? Imagine a life where each "yes" is given full-hearted attention, where each task is performed not out of hurried obligation but from a place of genuine engagement. This is the heart of not overcommitting. It is about knowing your capacities and honoring them, not just for your own health but for the integrity of everything you do. For the sake of living an integrated life!

In practice, not overcommitting means setting clear boundaries. It requires self-awareness to recognize when you are at capacity and the courage to communicate this to others. It is about prioritizing effectively, ensuring that your energies are spent on what truly matters, be it career ambitions, family life, personal growth, or other passions.

To implement this philosophy, start by evaluating your commitments. Which of these enhances your life, and which diminishes it? Learn the art of saying "no" with grace and conviction. Understand that each "no" to overcommitment is a "yes" to something else more valuable: more time with loved ones, more space for self-care, and more energy for the tasks that align with your personal and professional visions.

Once you embrace this concept, you will recognize that living this way is transformative. It will clear the clutter from your life, allowing you to breathe, focus, and excel. And in this clarity, there is a profound emotional and psychological uplift. The constant weight of pending tasks lifts, and what remains is a deeper satisfaction in your pursuits, a better quality of output, and a more joyful existence.

Not overcommitting does not mean standing still. It means moving forward with purpose and intention, knowing that your activities and responsibilities are not random or ill-considered but chosen precisely for their ability to enrich rather than deplete you.

This philosophy fosters an inner tranquility, knowing that you are doing your best in every aspect of your life that truly counts. It builds resilience, empowering you to face challenges without the crippling fear of failure because you have already set yourself on a path that is sustainable and rewarding.

Here are some questions that will help you do a quick self-assessment:

What are your beliefs about saying "no"? (start with "People who say "no" are...)

_____

_____

_____

_____

_____

What do you need to say "no" to right now?

_____

_____

_____

_____

_____

What currently stops you from saying "no"?

_____

_____

_____

_____

_____

The Art of saying no is fuel for success. In our fast-paced world, saying "yes" can often be a default setting. Have you considered the power of a well-placed "no"?

Reserve Tank. Think of yourself as a car. Even the most high-performance vehicles come with a reserve tank, a backup for when the primary fuel runs low. This reserve is your time, energy, and sanity. Guarded fearlessly because when it is gone, you will go nowhere. As discussed before, saying "no" is not an act of refusal but an act of self-preservation and a smart strategic approach. There will always be opportunities.

The key is to know when to embrace these opportunities without hesitation and when to hit the brakes for the sake of your reserves.

Recognizing the value of your expertise is essential. Equally, managing your energy and time effectively ensures that you do not become overwhelmed, which can tarnish your personal brand and hinder your growth. Remember to assess opportunities. Is it worth dipping into your reserves? Value your time. Your expertise is worth compensation. Manage your energy because overexertion benefits no one.

This concept has specifically helped me during a time in my career when I found myself committed to too many amazing things, from heading industry committees to being part of the PTA (Parent Teacher Association). Each commitment was intentionally designed to fill up a specific "cup" in my life. However, what is more important to understand is that there comes a time when some of these commitments have served their purpose. They expire. This is the time to reevaluate and gracefully bow out.

Here are some questions for self-reflection:

How do you determine when to say "yes" and when to say "no"? It is healthier. Choice?

_____

_____

_____

_____

_____

How are you protecting your reserve tank?

_____

_____

_____

_____

_____

Start making wiser choices that fuel your success and well-being today, and you will see the results tomorrow.

To live with 360° IMPACT integration and you can too! You must limit the amount of "yes" you give out to the world around you. Master your time management skills and make self-care a vehicle for massive productivity and the striving for work-life balance.

Not overcommitting means understanding life's rhythms, its recedes and flows, and aligning yourself with them rather than racing against them. It is to acknowledge that while the world often praises the busy, there is greater wisdom in praising the integrated, the thoughtful, and the passionately engaged.

Here lies the secret to not just surviving in this chaotic world but thriving within it.

By mastering this concept, you invite a more fulfilled, calm, and enriched life. Start embracing it wholeheartedly!

PROFESSIONAL APPLICATION

You feel exhausted from the endless pursuit of "work-life balance," and so does your team!

Prioritizing employee well-being and mental health should be as important to you as it should be to your team. Creating a supportive work environment is essential. Integrating diverse thinkers and people with special strengths into your team is more critical today than ever. Celebrating successes and fostering a culture of appreciation and gratitude must be at the forefront. Encouraging an integrated life and workplace is imperative. These are all necessary ingredients to providing your team with the space to operate in a more integrated workplace.

Research shows that leaders who are happy and feel fulfilled in their personal and professional lives inspire and encourage more effectively. Why? Because they have figured out how to live an integrated life, one that includes a little bit of everything they absolutely love. They excel at motivating their teams and make great mentors too!

Integrated leaders are happy leaders. And happy leaders make better leaders!

360° IMPACT leaders who choose integration over balance have a great sense of fairness and set high expectations. They also provide support and recognition for their teams to achieve those expectations.

Employee Well-being. A healthy workforce is essential for sustained success. 360° IMPACT leaders prioritize the well-being and mental health of their employees. By prioritizing the physical, mental, and emotional well-being of their employees, they promote a healthy, integrated life, provide access to resources and support, and foster a culture of self-care and resilience.

How I discovered the importance of well-being and mental health... Back in 2018, one beautiful morning in Las Vegas, after several years, the simple sound of birds chirping finally broke through the fog that had enveloped my life. I paused to breathe deeply, taking in the scent of blooming pear trees on a sunlit spring morning. This moment of tranquility was a stark contrast to the previous years, dominated by the relentless demands of my career. The intensity of this realization struck me profoundly, highlighting how disconnected I had become from all sensations of my everyday life.

This epiphany made me deeply aware of how much I had neglected not only my surroundings but also my relationships and personal well-being. My days had been consumed by a relentless pursuit of professional success, measured in endless metrics and achievements that now seemed so distant from what truly mattered. I had been so focused on client satisfaction, revenue, and performance indicators that I had overlooked the essential pleasures of life, like the warmth of the sun or the sounds of nature.

Reflecting on this, I understood that I had been experiencing severe burnout, a depletion so profound that it had extinguished my ability to engage fully with the world around me. Burnout is a topic we did not discuss enough until after the COVID-19 pandemic that shook us all.

It was alarming to realize that I could no longer remember the last time I had genuinely experienced life without the overlay of work and stress. The impact of this burnout extended beyond myself; it affected my family, too. I had been absent, physically present but mentally miles away, even during moments as simple and precious as listening to my oldest son's stories. This was a wake-up call, a realization that I needed to reclaim my health and happiness by reconnecting with the simple joys to nurture my mental and emotional well-being.

This story underscores the critical importance of mental health, especially in today's high-pressure world. Let it serve as a reminder that while ambition and hard work are valuable, they should not come at the cost of our health and happiness. And although my focus, discipline and effort paid off, there was a high-ticket to pay.

Taking time to enjoy life's simple pleasures, like the beauty of nature, and being fully present with your loved ones is not just rejuvenating but essential for your overall well-being. Let this be a lesson in the importance of balancing life's demands with self-care and mindfulness, ensuring you do not lose sight of what truly enriches you. That precious integration of every single aspect of your life.

For a 360° IMPACT on well-being, make this part of your culture, offer wellness programs and flexible work arrangements when possible, and make mental health resources available to support your team's overall happiness. And please, please, please, do not let them skip their days off or vacation time!

In fact, you want a radical idea? Make it mandatory! (more on this to come). This will add value to their desire to live a more fulfilled life! This is where you become a 360° IMPACT leader. **This** is where you start fostering a supportive work environment. Recognizing the importance of mental health and providing resources and support for employees to manage stress and maintain a high degree of resilience.

Provide access to counseling services, financial planning resources, or mental health support through an EAP (Employee Assistance Program) to assist employees during challenging times. Create a comfortable and inspiring work environment with ergonomic furniture, natural light, green spaces, healthy food choices, and designated relaxation areas to support physical and mental well-being. Encourage team-building activities, social events, or volunteer opportunities to strengthen relationships among employees and promote a sense of community. Offer financial education workshops, retirement planning assistance, or benefits like student loan repayment assistance to alleviate financial stress among employees. Provide resources for managing caregiving responsibilities, such as parental leave, childcare support, or eldercare assistance, to help employees balance work and personal life. Launch fun and engaging well-being challenges or campaigns focused on physical activity, healthy eating, mindfulness, or stress reduction to promote positive behaviors. Encourage employees to take regular breaks and utilize their vacation days.

I advised you this was coming. I want to stop on this last one for a minute. It is data sharing time! YAY! (do not roll your eyes, please). According to surveys, many employees in the United States do not fully utilize their vacation days. One study found that, on average, Americans used only about 54% of their eligible vacation time in 2021. Meanwhile, employees in European countries often use a higher percentage of their vacation entitlement. For example, workers in France and Germany typically take most or all of their annual vacation days.

The amount of vacation time provided to employees varies by country.

France is renowned for its stringent labor laws that prioritize employee welfare. French labor laws mandate a minimum of five weeks of paid vacation per year. Additionally, the country has implemented policies that encourage employees to fully disconnect from work during their time off, fostering a healthier work-life balance.

Germany's approach to mandatory paid vacation is equally impressive. Employees are entitled to a minimum of 20 paid vacation days annually, and it is a common practice for companies to encourage employees to utilize all their allotted vacation days. German employers understand that a well-rested workforce is key to maintaining the country's strong economic performance.

In Japan, the government has taken proactive steps to address the cultural norm of overworking by implementing laws that require employees to take at least five days of paid leave each year. This policy aims to combat the nation's infamous "karoshi" (death by overwork) phenomenon and promote a healthier, more balanced lifestyle.

Brazil mandates that employees take 30 consecutive days of paid vacation annually. This policy not only supports employee well-being but also promotes a culture where taking time off is normalized and valued.

Argentina exemplifies the importance of mandatory paid vacation with laws ensuring employees take substantial breaks to boost well-being and productivity. Workers with up to 5 years of service get 14 consecutive days of paid vacation, those with 5-10 years receive 21 days, 10-20 years are granted 28 days, and over 20 years earn 35 days. This policy promotes comprehensive rest, enhances work-life balance, and increases productivity, demonstrating a profound cultural commitment to employee well-being and setting a compelling model for other nations to follow.

Ready for the closing act? Keep reading.

In stark contrast to many developed nations, the United States remains one of the few without federal laws mandating paid vacation, leaving millions of workers at the mercy of their employers' discretion. On average, Americans scrape by with a mere 10 days of paid vacation **after** one year of service, woefully less than their global counterparts.

This glaring absence of mandatory time off fuels a culture of relentless work, leading to poor work-life balance, skyrocketing stress, and diminished productivity. Despite the ingrained belief that longer hours equate to higher output, studies reveal that well-rested employees are the true powerhouses of innovation and efficiency.

America, where generations have been groomed to prioritize productivity over downtime.

By making well-being a priority and mandating downtime, in other words, encouraging team members to take the time allotted to them, you prevent them having to address "the big elephant in the room". Cultural attitudes toward taking vacations can influence employees' behavior. In some countries, taking time off is seen as essential for well-being and productivity. In others, there may be stigma or pressure associated with taking extended vacations or frequent time off. In fact, in some countries in Europe, it is considered inappropriate or even tacky to discuss work-related matters after the workday is over.

To make a 360° IMPACT, employee well-being must be integrated into your organizational culture and must be recognized as critical to long-term success.

Inclusive Work Environment. In recent years, organizations worldwide have increasingly invested in diversity, equity, and inclusion (DEI) initiatives, and the results have varied. Ella Washington, an organizational psychologist and professor at Georgetown University's McDonough School of Business, emphasizes the need for sustained commitment to this work for meaningful and lasting change. Based on her research, Washington identifies five stages of DEI maturity:

- Aware
- Compliant
- Tactical
- Integrated
- Sustainable

Each requires considerable time and effort to navigate. She delves into why certain organizations encounter obstacles and offers insights on how to surmount these challenges. Washington's expertise is detailed in her book, "The Necessary Journey: Making Real Progress on Equity and Inclusion," (published in 2022) and her Harvard Business Review article, "The Five Stages of DEI Maturity." This framework provides a roadmap for organizations striving to progress towards genuine DEI transformation.

Many organizations are drawn to bold DEI initiatives inspired by other companies, but often, these efforts lack sustainability and meaningful impact. DEI work requires a long-term commitment to cultural change and structural readiness. Rushing into grand gestures without proper foundations can lead to failure and undermine trust in the company's intentions.

We must have diversity, inclusion, and belonging to create a culture where humans feel like humans and where we promote a life of integration.

Why do we tend to overcomplicate this? It is not that difficult to create a place where people feel they can be authentic and feel supported for whatever difference "defined" them. We must start by remembering what it is to be human and by fostering tolerance. Biases and stereotypes must be challenged. It is by learning about everyone's differences, the ones that are evident to the eye and those which are not.

This is the most compelling way to continue to move the needle towards building a better world for the generations to come. A world with 360° IMPACT integration!

Tolerance and compassion are qualities that can make you a 360° IMPACT leader. Whether you lead team members or not. According to Theodore Roosevelt, people do not care how much you know until they know how much you care. So, integrate tolerance and compassion into your life and become a better human.

Many moons back, I started researching and studying the topic of DEI. At the time, my research focus was on understanding generational and cultural differences in order to create better standards for the workplace. What prompted this journey was a very special project I was working on. This project involved assisting a department head in implementing significant changes within an underperforming department.

A struggling housekeeping department in a bustling hotel. The atmosphere was charged with frustration and miscommunication. The staff, spanning from Traditionalists (although just a few) to Millennials, seemed disconnected by differing values and work styles. My goal was simple yet ambitious: create a harmonious and efficient team environment by leveraging these generational differences rather than allowing them to be a point of contention.

Four generations under one roof! Sounds like fun, right?!

How about we add a little spice to it and say, all from different areas of the world. Yeah! Why not?!

One of the initiatives was specific to targeting generational differences. I initiated the project by carefully analyzing the existing dynamics and then introducing strategies that catered uniquely to the needs of each generation. Recognizing the diverse communication styles. I implemented a dual-channel approach: maintaining traditional face-to-face meetings for those who valued personal interaction and integrating digital tools for those who thrived on technological efficiency. This hybrid system bridged the gap between them, fostering a new level of understanding and respect among the team members.

To capitalize on the varied strengths across generations, I organized cross-generational training workshops. These sessions were eye-opening, as they not only facilitated skill-sharing but also helped build mutual respect and empathy among the team members. The younger employees took the lead on technology, bringing their older colleagues up to speed with digital scheduling, spending tracking, and inventory management tools. Conversely, the more experienced staff shared invaluable customer service insights, communication strategies, and work ethics that enriched the professional growth of the younger team members. There was absolute integration!

Another significant change was the introduction of flexible work schedules, which addressed the lifestyle preferences across the workforce. This flexibility was particularly well-received by the Millennial employees, who cherished work-life balance as a result of living with parents who were constantly at work. And, also appreciated by the older employees who found new vigor in a more adaptable approach to traditional work hours, after working. Many Baby Boomers were raised (in many cases by Traditionalists) with the idea that job stability and company loyalty were paramount. Where the conventional

9:00-to-5:00 workday was the norm. This new initiative opened a gateway to a new universe for Traditionalists and Baby Boomers, where they could color a little outside the lines.

The culmination of these efforts was a revamped recognition program. We moved beyond the conventional "employee of the month" framework, incorporating acknowledgments that resonated with personal and professional growth opportunities. This new recognition strategy not only boosted morale but also drove all team members to embrace innovation and efficiency in their daily tasks.

The transformation was profound, to say the least. Within months, there was a noticeable improvement in morale and productivity. Employee engagement scores soared, and this renewed vigor was evident in the quality of their work. Customer feedback became overwhelmingly positive, highlighting the attentiveness and dedication of the housekeeping staff. The department that was once the weakest link in the hotel's operations had become a model of efficiency and teamwork.

Absolute integration!

This success story is a testament to the power of embracing diversity within the workplace. By recognizing and valuing the unique contributions of each age group, the housekeeping department not only turned its performance around but also set a standard for other departments within the hotel. It was a clear demonstration that when people feel understood and valued, they connect not just with their work but with each other, leading to outstanding operational success.

If you want to be a 360° IMPACT leader, embrace everyone's differences by educating yourself. This education will help you understand and appreciate the rich and colorful human backgrounds, perspectives, disabilities, and experiences, fostering a more inclusive and equitable society. It is no secret that people want to feel included. Celebrate diversity and inclusion, and make an effort to create a sense of belonging for everyone.

Here is an analogy for you:

- Diversity is when everyone gets an invitation to the party.
- Equity is like being given an opportunity to get out on the dance floor.
- Inclusion is being invited to dance.
- Belonging is when everyone has a chance to choose the music being played.

360° IMPACT Leaders integrate a sense of belonging by actively seeking out and addressing systemic barriers to inclusion, creating opportunities for all team members to thrive.

Neurodiversity And Disabilities. The inclusion of neurodiversity and disabilities in the workplace is not only a matter of social justice or compliance with legal standards. It also brings substantial benefits that enhance innovation, productivity, and workplace culture. 360° IMPACT leaders understand the importance of embracing neurodiversity and disabilities and the advantages this brings to any organization. It is the right thing to do.

What I have experienced is that when discussing diversity, equity, and inclusion (DEI), it is common to focus primarily on factors like race, gender, and age. While these dimensions are crucial components of DEI efforts, it is important to recognize that diversity encompasses a much broader spectrum of identities and experiences. Beyond race and gender, diversity includes aspects such as disability status, socioeconomic background, neurodiversity, religious beliefs, veteran status, and more. Each of these dimensions contributes to the richness of human diversity and presents unique challenges and opportunities for inclusion.

People who are neurodiverse or have disabilities often bring unique perspectives that can lead to novel ideas and solutions. They are The Master of Resilience. Their different ways of processing information and solving problems can add valuable insights that might not arise from neurotypical or non-disabled employees. This diversity of thought can be crucial in creative problem-solving and can drive innovation within teams, leading to new products, services, or ways of working that can differentiate a company in the marketplace.

Individuals with physical disabilities or who are neurodiverse often develop unique skills by adapting to a world not designed for their needs. Individuals with disabilities possess extraordinary abilities and unique strengths that many of us can only dream of acquiring. For example, someone with autism might have extraordinary abilities in pattern recognition, memory, or concentration on specific tasks. While someone with a physical disability might have developed strong problem-solving skills or the ability to use technology in innovative ways.

Temple Grandin, diagnosed with autism in childhood, has become a transformative figure in animal science and a leading advocate for the autism community. As a professor of animal science at Colorado State University and a consultant on animal behavior, she has revolutionized livestock handling with her designs, which improve animal welfare and industry efficiency by considering animal perspectives. Grandin also promotes a greater understanding of autism through her writing and speaking, emphasizing the unique contributions of neurodiverse individuals. Her work exemplifies the profound impact of embracing and understanding neurodiversity in professional and social contexts.

Brad Smith is the President of Microsoft and has been a key leader in the company's growth and innovation. Brad has a physical disability known as Charcot-Marie-Tooth (CMT) disease, which affects his mobility and requires the use of crutches or a scooter for mobility. Despite his disability, Brad Smith has played a pivotal role in shaping Microsoft's strategic direction and initiatives. He is known for his advocacy for diversity and inclusion within the tech industry, emphasizing the importance of accessibility in technology products and services. In the workplace, Brad Smith's leadership and insights have influenced Microsoft's commitment to creating accessible technologies for people with disabilities. Under his leadership, Microsoft has developed innovative accessibility features in its products, such as Windows, Office, and Xbox, making technology more inclusive and efficient for users of all abilities.

There are millions of examples like these. This highlights how these individuals can bring valuable perspectives and drive positive change within well-known organizations, leading to more inclusive and efficient workplaces that benefit everyone. Harnessing these skills can provide companies with a competitive edge.

My experience working with team members who had a visible or non-visible "disability" has been not only enriching but also enlightening.

Early in my career, with conviction in my theory and a load of determination, throughout the years, I tested the approach of promoting the hiring of more team members with visible and non-visible "disabilities" by creating strategic partnerships with specific organizations. This later became a company best-practice in all markets.

I can recall one team member at a project in Las Vegas, Nevada, who was on the autistic spectrum and required substantial support to communicate and deal with change. This team member, among other qualities, was kind, focused on the task, never missed a day of work, and became extremely loyal to the brand. It was team members like him and many others, who propelled me to make it my life-long mission to advocate for this to become a best practice in all organizations. This advocacy involves a range of strategies, from raising awareness and educating staff to implementing practical changes in the workplace. From this point forward, my message consistently drives focus on connecting with people in a more human way!

Little did I know that one day, this would be a mission that would hit home in a different way. An unforeseen connection to the mission.

It takes intention to choose to have a 360° IMPACT integrated team, and you do not have to do it alone. Seek partnership with organizations like *Best Buddies International*, whose mission is to establish a global volunteer movement that creates opportunities for one-to-one friendships, integrated employment, leadership development, inclusive living, and family support for individuals with intellectual and developmental disabilities. Or like *In Good Company Works*, whose mission is to help businesses adapt to a changing workforce with inclusive employment practices that empower employers to hire and retain employees with intellectual and developmental disabilities.

Studies have proven that workers with disabilities are often more reliable and have better job retention rates compared to their non-disabled counterparts. They are less likely to take sick days or engage in job hopping. This can lead to reduced turnover and lower costs related to hiring and training new staff. Employees with disabilities frequently demonstrate high levels of commitment and loyalty, appreciating the opportunity to work in an inclusive environment. And they have BIG hearts!

To become a 360° IMPACT leader, be committed to this new level of diversity and inclusion. This will attract not only potential employees but also customers who prefer to support companies with strong social values. Demonstrate inclusivity concerning employees with disabilities and neurodiverse individuals and expand your company's customer base to include these communities and their allies. But do it because it is the right thing to do, not to just check a box!

Inclusive workplaces where diversity is valued tend to exhibit better team dynamics and higher overall employee morale. When all employees feel valued and included, it fosters a positive work environment that benefits everyone.

Inclusive cultures encourage mutual respect and minimize toxic workplace behaviors, leading to more effective teamwork and increased productivity.

By actively recruiting and supporting workers with disabilities and those who are neurodiverse, you can tap into a wider pool of talent. This approach will allow you to find the best person for the job who might otherwise be overlooked due to outdated standard hiring practices that do not accommodate diverse needs.

A 360° IMPACT integrated approach to DEI not only strengthens the workforce but also mirrors a broader commitment to embracing diversity as a source of strength and competitive advantage. And the bonus, you become a contributing participant in creating a more colorful world!

Recognition And Celebration. Experiencing happiness, fulfillment, and appreciation in the workplace is crucial for achieving an integrated life. As discussed before, when you are not happy at work, it will affect all other areas of your life.

360° IMPACT leaders prioritize celebrating successes and milestones, honoring both individual and team contributions. They facilitate opportunities for joy and fulfillment through team-building activities, social gatherings, and collective celebrations. They cultivate a culture of appreciation and gratitude by publicly acknowledging achievements and offering meaningful rewards and advancement opportunities. This approach not only reinforces positive behavior but also boosts morale, strengthens team cohesion, and ensures that everyone feels valued and recognized within the organization.

Your role as a 360° IMPACT leader is pivotal, not just in steering the organization toward its goals but in creating a sense of collective joy and shared success. At the core of this leadership style is the profound understanding that a workplace thrives when its people do, not merely in terms of productivity but in their sense of belonging, achievement, and joy.

The lifeblood of every successful organization pulses the heartbeats of its team members, each contributing to the rhythm of progress and innovation. As a 360° IMPACT leader, you have a duty to recognize these efforts and transform routine milestones into moments of collective celebration. When a project reaches fruition or a quarterly target is met, push yourself to see beyond the numbers and charts and instead, see the late hours, the problem-solving, the teamwork, and most importantly, the personal sacrifices.

This approach does not just make the workplace a venue for professional growth, but a garden where personal and collective well-being flourishes.

In a culture of appreciation crafted by a 360° IMPACT leader, recognition is thoughtful and resonant. Public acknowledgments during meetings, awards that signify real appreciation, or even promotions and professional development opportunities, each act of recognition is tailored to genuinely value the individual's contribution. This is not about ticking boxes on a corporate checklist; it is about genuinely understanding and valuing what each team member brings to the table. It is about making them feel seen, heard, and valued. And if you want to take this approach further, learn how each individual contributor would like to be recognized and celebrated and tailor it to them. For instance, celebrating an introverted team member in public may not be the way to go. Although your intention is good, their desire to disappear or hide under a desk can make this recognition lose its value.

When you start creating this type of cultural shift, success will never be solitary. Every achievement will be a mosaic of many hands and hearts. When one team member excels, you will fundamentally ensure that this success is celebrated as a collective triumph, reinforcing the idea that each individual's success contributes to the legacy of the whole team. This will foster an environment of mutual support and encouragement, where everyone is motivated to contribute their best, knowing that their efforts will be recognized and even celebrated.

The emotional resonance of this approach cannot be understated. In a world often bogged down by targets and deadlines, these moments of recognition and celebration are like breaths of fresh air; they rejuvenate and inspire. Employees feel emotionally connected to their workplace, not just as a place to work but as a community that values their well-being and celebrates their contributions.

This emotional bond is what transforms average teams into extraordinary ones, fostering a workplace where innovation, loyalty, and joy are the norm, not the exception.

Key takeaways: 360° IMPACT integration is characterized by a combination of self-respect, setting boundaries, and watching your reserve tank. By prioritizing employee well-being and mental health, offering flexibility and support for work-life integration, fostering inclusivity and diversity, and recognizing and celebrating successes, 360° IMPACT leaders can create an environment where individuals thrive professionally and personally.

CHAPTER 6

COLLABORATION
Driving change and innovation

Adding collaboration to your toolbox!

In the grand tapestry of human achievement, woven through the chronicles of history and innovation, there lies a golden thread that has persistently defined the success of every monumental venture: collaboration. It is the silent heartbeat behind the most seismic shifts in our world, the unsung hero in the narratives of those who have reshaped boundaries and redefined eras. Today, as we stand on the precipice of new possibilities and confront challenges that stretch the limits of our imagination, the call for collaboration has never been louder or clearer.

It is not just an option but a necessity, a fundamental driver of change and innovation.

Consider the moments that have defined progress: the moon landings, the digital revolution, the breakthroughs in medicine and science. None of these were the triumphs of lone warriors; they were victories forged through the fire of collective effort, diverse expertise, and shared vision. The genius behind collaboration is that it multiplies our individual capacities exponentially. It transforms personal limitations into collective strengths, melding the best of us into something greater than the sum of our parts.

The emotional resonance of collaboration is profound. It speaks to our innate desire to connect, to belong, to contribute to something larger than ourselves. This drive, deeply embedded in our nature, is what has propelled societies forward. What has turned fledgling startups into global giants and simple ideas into revolutionary technologies? In the realm of collaboration, each participant becomes both a teacher and a student. Both a mentor and an apprentice are engaged in the dual act of giving and receiving that is central to human growth and satisfaction.

However, to view collaboration through the glowing tint of idealism would be an oversight. True collaboration is not a path empty of obstacles; rather, it is a journey marked by challenges that require not just skill but heart. It demands empathy, patience, and the courage to trust others with your visions and dreams.

It asks of leaders not to stand above but among, not to direct but to inspire, not to constantly compete but to create "Blue Oceans"*.

[*"Blue Ocean Strategy," written by W. Chan Kim and Renée Mauborgne, is a groundbreaking business book that introduces the concept of creating uncontested market space, or "blue oceans," rather than competing in saturated markets, or "red oceans." The authors argue that businesses can succeed not by battling competitors but by creating new, untapped market spaces filled with opportunities. If you have not read it, I highly recommend you do (first published in 2005).]

This narrative of collaboration as the driver of innovation and change unfolds in every successful community, team, company, and movement. From the kitchen table where the family gathers at the end of each day and the cluttered garages where startups were born to the sleek boardrooms of global enterprises, the principle holds true: *when minds meet with openness and ambition, the potential for greatness increases.*

It is about creating spaces where voices are not only heard but valued, where the clash of ideas is not a battleground but a crucible for creativity.

Think of the world's most successful innovator, the late Steve Jobs, who once said, "Great things in business are never done by one person.

They're done by a team of people." He knew the immense power of gathering around him people who could challenge and complement his vision. Or consider the story of Lin-Manuel Miranda, who created the groundbreaking musical "Hamilton" by collaborating with historians, musicians, actors, and choreographers, weaving together a tapestry of talents to tell a story that captivated the world.

In every sector, whether technology, healthcare, education, or the arts, the stories of breakthrough success are stories of collaboration. They are about breaking down silos, bridging gaps, and building bonds. This collaborative spirit extends beyond the workplace into our personal lives, echoing the sense of community found in churches, neighborhoods, and social circles. Just as churches and community gatherings foster a sense of belonging and shared purpose, successful organizations embrace collaboration to achieve common goals and foster innovation.

Recognizing that in the diversity of our experiences, strengths, and expertise lies our greatest strength.

You see, the magic of collaboration extends beyond achieving external success; it transforms us internally. It molds our character, teaches us humility, and expands our perspectives. It shows us the power of putting collective goals above individual glory, connecting with others on a deeper level, and the joy of seeing others succeed alongside us. This is the essence of being human.

A human who understands that its brightest flame is kindled not by one but by many.

As you prepare to delve deeper into the power of collaboration presented in this chapter, imagine the possibilities that await when we combine our strengths and dreams. Think of the innovations lying dormant, just waiting for the right partnership to bring them to life.

Consider the global challenges that could be overcome if we truly learned to work together, transcending borders, sectors, and differences.

This exploration is not just about understanding a concept but about reimagining the way we operate in every facet of our lives. It is about building bridges where there are walls, about seeing the "other" not as a competitor but as a partner in the quest for a better world. It invites you to be a part of this transformative journey, to be a leader who drives change not by sheer force of will but by the inspiring art of collaboration.

Prepare to be moved, to be inspired, and to see the world and your role within it through a new lens, one where collaboration is not just a strategy but the very essence of success. Let's explore how, through the collective power of our efforts, ideas, differences, and spirits, we can not only imagine but create a world that is more colorful than anything we could accomplish alone.

John C. Maxwell presents the concept that no leader has ever done anything on their own. Looking back in time, I notice that every successful person always had a sidekick or a team working toward the cause.

We live in an era defined by collaboration. More and more people from diverse backgrounds and industries are coming together in innovative ways. Artists collaborate across disciplines, merging music, visual arts, and technology to create immersive experiences that transcend traditional boundaries. Brands are partnering with influencers and content creators to reach new audiences and co-create engaging content that resonates with consumers. In the tech sector, startups collaborate with established companies to leverage expertise and resources, driving innovation and disrupting industries. Beyond business, educators collaborate with technology experts to develop interactive learning platforms that enhance student engagement and outcomes. Hotel brands collaborate with other brands through co-branding, culinary partnerships, travel and transportation deals, wellness and fitness collaborations, entertainment events, technology integrations, retail experiences, and sustainability initiatives. These partnerships enhance guest experiences, differentiate the hotel, and provide unique, memorable services. Even in social impact initiatives, nonprofits collaborate with corporations and government agencies to tackle complex challenges like sustainability and social justice. Additionally, parents are joining forces, sharing knowledge and support to navigate the demands of parenting, fostering a sense of community and mutual assistance.

This era of collaboration is demonstrating the power of collective creativity and shared goals, leading to unprecedented advancements and positive change in our interconnected world.

PERSONAL APPLICATION

Personal Board Of Directors. No one has to walk their life journey alone. We must all start embracing the age of collaboration. And to do so, you must build your personal "Board of Directors." Companies have them and you should too. Because having your own personal board of directors is not just a luxury, but a necessity.

Imagine a world where competition is replaced with collective triumph. Where seasoned mentors, peers and even friends become the architects of each other's achievements. This is what I mean when I say, "build your board of directors" or "toolbox".

This consists of individuals who do not only celebrate with you but also are not afraid to deliver a reality check when you veer off course. They are your cheerleaders, your strategists, and sometimes the much-needed voice of tough love. Especially when the daunting imposter syndrome casts its shadow over your confidence. They are your safe space, free from judgment, where vulnerability isn't a weakness but a shared strength. Your board of directors is where you will find someone whispering your name into the universe of opportunities, helping you shine brighter than you could alone.

Grounded, understood, and with your sanity intact, that is how you will feel with a powerful group of people around you. Because they GET YOU! Just as you understand and support them in return.

I am immensely grateful for my personal board of directors, a diverse group of incredible people who contribute uniquely to my journey as a leader of my life. To each of you, THANK YOU!

Now, it is your turn! Create a list of who they are and make time to thank them. Think of everything you have experienced with them. Think of all the times they have helped along the way.

Come up with at least 5 names:

_____

_____

_____

_____

_____

How have they propelled you towards your goals?

_____

_____

_____

_____

_____

How do you contribute to the growth of others in your own board?

_____

_____

_____

_____

_____

Find your people, grow together, and lift each other up!

Creating a personal board of directors specifically aimed at enhancing your personal life involves assembling a trusted group of advisors who can guide you through life's various challenges and opportunities. This concept is about choosing individuals who can offer wisdom, emotional support, and insight into making life choices that align with your personal values, aspirations, and well-being.

In order to ensure that there is alignment, start by reflecting deeply on what matters most to you in your personal life. This might include your family, health, spiritual growth, personal development, or community involvement. Start with your purpose, as described in Chapter 3. Clearly defining your values and goals will serve as the foundation for selecting members of your personal board.

Look for individuals who embody the personal qualities you admire and aspire towards. These might be family members - those who know you well and have always had your best interests at heart, mentors - people who have guided you in the past or whose wisdom you respect; peers - friends or colleagues who inspire you with their approach to life and personal integrity, professionals - therapists, coaches, or spiritual leaders who can offer expert advice in their respective areas.

Identify who can be empathetic and offer emotional support during tough times. Determine who can provide honest, unbiased feedback on your personal decisions. Consider who consistently motivates you and believes in your potential.

When considering the concept of creating a personal board of directors or a close group of collaborators, the principles of open communication are equally crucial. This group, much like a corporate board, can help guide your personal and professional decisions, offering advice, support, and accountability.

Encourage a culture where all thoughts, feedback, and challenges can be shared openly without judgment. This transparency is key to building trust and allows for more creative and effective problem-solving in your community, your household, and your workplace. When your collaborators feel secure in sharing their insights and feedback, you gain the full benefit of their expertise and diverse perspectives, which enables you to grow at a faster speed.

Here are a few reflection questions for you to work on:

How do you currently collaborate with others around you?

_____

_____

_____

_____

What do you need to do today to have a well-crafted personal "Board of Directors"?

_____

_____

_____

_____

_____

Like-minded People. Collaborating with like-minded individuals is a deeply fulfilling and transformative experience that goes beyond mere social interaction. It taps into a fundamental human need for understanding, support, and belonging. When you find people who share your passions and challenges, there is an instant sense of connection and empathy that cannot be overstated. It is like discovering a community that speaks your language—the language of shared dreams, aspirations, and struggles.

These relationships offer more than just camaraderie; they become pillars of strength in your journey. They elevate your game!

Imagine having a circle of individuals who not only comprehend your goals but also actively cheer you on and offer guidance when the path gets tough. Those whose stories of perseverance and success inspire you to keep pushing forward, even when obstacles seem insurmountable. This kind of encouragement is invaluable, fueling your motivation and instilling a sense of accountability that propels you toward your aspirations.

Collaborating with like-minded people positively impacts every facet of your life. When you engage with a community that shares your passions, you feel validated, understood, and empowered. These connections transcend the superficial—they become transformative forces that enrich your journey and contribute to your growth and fulfillment.

To collaborate on a 360° IMPACT level, seek out these meaningful connections, cherish them, and watch how they elevate your life to new heights. Surround yourself with like-minded people who will move you out of your comfort zone by inviting you to think differently.

When you are in circles where you feel like you are learning nothing and these circles no longer add value, it is time for change!

If the room feels small, find a bigger room!

Engage in a mastermind group, a collaborative network of individuals with diverse skills and perspectives focused on personal or professional growth. This group can meet regularly to discuss goals, share insights, provide feedback, and hold each other accountable.

At Kline Hospitality, our masterminds are called "Connection Labs." These spaces are transformative arenas where the magic of deep and purposeful conversations unfolds. Here, diverse groups of individuals, each with their unique stories and perspectives, converge with a shared passion for personal evolution. It is a sanctuary for elevated dissertations—a departure from the ordinary—where participants delve into different yet relevant topics. In these moments, connections are forged, and spirits are lifted.

Meaningful exchanges elevate souls and foster genuine human connection. It is the real, unfiltered dialogues that stir inspiration and propel lives toward purpose-driven paths. These spaces are where the ordinary transforms into the extraordinary, one conversation at a time.

In masterminds like these, members lean in, share best practices, and strengthen a bond that holds them together: common ground. Conversations require listening by being fully present. They require collaboration from all parties involved. Deep listening builds trust in relationships.

Shameless plug about our Connection Labs: Our topic-driven, meaningful conversations give our members social support and a moment in time to stop the "busy hamster wheel" they are caught in and reflect. In our Maxwell Leadership masterminds, we provide our clients with an opportunity to choose from an array of books. During these programs our clients learn about developing themselves (and others) so that they have the best chance at becoming the person they were created to be.

The benefits of finding collaboration in a mastermind setting are endless. Mastermind groups create a supportive environment where members contribute knowledge and resources, fostering personal development and achievement. Participants pool their expertise and resources, offering diverse perspectives and solutions to individual challenges. Regular meetings and goal-setting within the group encourage accountability and drive progress toward personal objectives. Members provide constructive feedback and emotional support, facilitating self-improvement and resilience. Mastermind groups offer networking opportunities, connecting individuals to new ideas, opportunities, and potential collaborations.

Community Outreach. Getting involved in community service or volunteer initiatives is not just about giving back; it is a deeply emotional and enriching experience that connects individuals to something larger than themselves. The act of collaborating with others in community projects can be transformative, both for the community and the individual.

When you engage in community outreach that is aligned with your personal interests or values, you embark on a journey that goes beyond mere service; it becomes a shared mission. Imagine a passionate environmentalist joining a local tree-planting initiative or a healthcare professional volunteering at a free Clinic for underserved populations. These individuals are not just offering their time; they are investing their hearts and souls into causes that resonate deeply with them.

A great example of how community outreach fosters collaboration is seen in Habitat for Humanity, an organization that brings together volunteers from various backgrounds to build homes for families in need. Participants work side by side, sharing skills and resources to create tangible solutions that directly impact the lives of others. Through this collaborative effort, volunteers develop lasting bonds and a profound sense of accomplishment.

Another example is community gardens, where neighbors come together to grow food collectively. These projects not only promote sustainability but also cultivate a sense of unity and mutual support. Participants share knowledge, tools, and labor, transforming vacant lots into vibrant, productive spaces that benefit the entire neighborhood.

Something magical happened to me a few years ago. I was invited to speak at Dress For Success of Southern Nevada to the women they serve. The objective was for me to inspire them through my story outlined in the book "Becoming an Unstoppable Woman." To help them get inspired that hardship is temporary and a great source of learning and growth. I shared the highlights and honed in on my areas of learning. Everyone took a copy with them. Throughout the day, I had engaged with over 40 women in only a few hours of being there. What a treat!!!

At the end of the event, a lady came up to me with a little girl. She must have been seven years old. The girl looked straight into my eyes with intensity and started to talk. This was back in 2021 when we were still required to wear masks, so communicating with our eyes was significant. She said: *"You know I'm Latina too, and I'm a speaker too, and I never met a Latina speaker with whom I could relate."*

Seven years old!!! Her mother was overwhelmed with tears of happiness. And quite frankly, I was too. This is the magic of a two way 360° IMPACT.

I then asked her: *"what do you want to be when you are a little older than now?"* (I wanted to ensure that she felt included regardless of the age gap with the group), and she said: *"I want to be a writer."* Her voice was filled with excitement, passion, and emotion. I then asked her: *"What would you like to write about?"* Not expecting an answer from her, she immediately replied, *"I want to write books for kids who need to be happy."* My heart melted!

I encouraged her to get a little notebook so that she could start putting her thoughts to paper right away.

We underestimate the power of collaboration in our community. The exposure that the little girl received that day was priceless.

Collaborating in community projects enriches personal growth by exposing individuals to diverse perspectives and challenges. It's a chance to learn new skills, refine leadership abilities, and gain a broader understanding of societal issues. Through these experiences, individuals often discover a deeper sense of purpose and fulfillment as they witness the positive impact of their collective efforts on the well-being of others.

Community outreach is not just about lending a helping hand; it is about forging connections, nurturing passions, and building bridges of understanding.

It is about creating a 360° IMPACT in our society! And, we are all responsible for this.

Start making a 360° IMPACT through collaboration in volunteer work so that you not only contribute to societal good but also embark on a deeply meaningful journey of personal and communal growth.

Experience the journey that unfolds with each shared experience, each new relationship formed, and each life touched. A 360° IMPACT journey that leaves a lasting imprint on both the giver and the receiver.

Collaboration leads to innovation because it is teamwork that makes the dream work!

PROFESSIONAL APPLICATION

Effective collaboration is instrumental in navigating the challenges of embracing disruption and leading through change. By bringing together diverse perspectives and experiences, collaborative teams can harness the power of collective creativity to generate innovative ideas that address evolving needs and market dynamics.

When "I" is replaced with "we," even illness becomes wellness.

Encouraging a culture of openness and experimentation within these teams creates valuable opportunities to learn from failure and refine strategies in response to feedback and unexpected outcomes. Building agile and adaptive teams through collaboration enables organizations to navigate uncertainty with resilience and agility, leveraging each member's strengths to drive continuous improvement and success in dynamic environments. In essence, collaboration not only strengthens teamwork but also cultivates a mindset that thrives on change, creativity, and the pursuit of new possibilities.

This concept of effective collaboration serves as a cornerstone for organizations seeking to thrive in environments defined by change, creativity and innovation, agility and adaptability, and continuous improvement. When fostering collaboration, teams are better equipped to embrace disruption and lead through change by leveraging diverse perspectives to anticipate shifts in market trends and customer needs. This collaborative approach encourages creativity and innovation by providing a platform for sharing and refining novel ideas, sparking new solutions to emerging challenges.

Moreover, embracing collaboration promotes agility and adaptability within teams, enabling them to respond swiftly and effectively to evolving circumstances. Through continuous improvement cycles driven by collaborative efforts, organizations can iteratively enhance processes, products, and services to meet evolving demands better and exceed expectations. Ultimately, the adaptive nature of collaborative teams empowers organizations to navigate uncertainty with confidence, turning change into an opportunity for growth and innovation.

Change. Our ability to embrace change can be significantly enhanced through collaboration. 360° IMPACT leaders embrace change as a natural part of growth and innovation. Cultivate a culture of agility and adaptability, where individuals are encouraged to experiment, learn, and evolve. 360° IMPACT Leaders embrace change as a catalyst for growth and transformation!

When you foster a culture where experimentation is encouraged, failure is normalized, and learning is celebrated.

Once you turn your focus to embracing change as an opportunity for growth and innovation, you will create a culture where experimentation and risk-taking are encouraged. Where collaboration thrives, you will unsurprisingly foster an environment where failure is seen as a natural part of the learning process and opportunities for growth.

A few years ago, I found myself in the midst of a tumultuous divorce and custody battle while simultaneously leading a large division with over 2,000 employees, and under the rule of a challenging boss. Reflecting on these experiences, I have come to view them as blessings in disguise, not because they were easy, but because they taught me invaluable lessons about resilience and strength. About embracing change, and most importantly, about the power of collaboration in times of change!

Rather than seeing setbacks as failures, I embrace them as opportunities for growth and learning. Just like you, life presented me with unexpected challenges, several relocations across the world, professional obstacles, and personal desires that seemed elusive. Through it all, I refused to give up. Instead, I accepted each challenge as a chance to expand my capabilities and push beyond my perceived limits.

And I did not do it alone.

It was the power of collaboration that allowed me to navigate through these challenges, drawing support and insights from colleagues, mentors, and friends who helped me see the path forward and find strength in adversity. This collaborative effort enabled me to not only survive but thrive, emerging from these trials with newfound perspective and determination to embrace change and resilience in all aspects of life and leadership.

Looking back on these experiences, I recall asking life if I could catch a break, only to realize that each trial was preparing me for something greater. Life's challenges became ingredients in a complex recipe, shaping me into an unstoppable force.

Rather than dwelling on the difficulties, put on your superhero attire, ask for help from others, and delve into the power of change as a driver of resilience and determination. In your journey to become a 360° IMPACT leader, help your team understand the concept of embracing change, too. In the face of doubt, remember that choosing to win or learn is more powerful than succumbing to fear of failure. So, embrace change with courage and conviction, seizing each challenge as an opportunity to grow and thrive. Communicate the rationale behind change initiatives and provide support and resources for implementation. And, lean into the power of collaboration.

As a 360° IMPACT leader your role is to cultivate an environment where thinking outside the box is not just welcomed but celebrated.

Encourage your team to collaborate with each other. To generate and explore new ideas fearlessly, recognizing that innovation thrives on diversity of thought and fearless exploration.

Create opportunities for collaborative brainstorming sessions, where the collective energy and creativity of your team can ignite sparks of innovation. This stage is where ideas are born, shaped, and refined through spirited discussions and collective insights. Embrace the chaos of creativity and provide the platform for your team to explore, ideate, and collaborate freely. Move collaboration from a simple concept to a fundamental aspect of your team's identity.

When your team starts collaborating, they will rise to the challenge of pushing boundaries, sparking innovation, and driving meaningful change within your organization.

Together, you can unleash the full potential of each team member, and foster a culture where innovation becomes a way of life. An inspiring journey of discovery and growth.

Charles Darwin once said: "It is not the strongest of the species that survive, nor the most intelligent, but the one most responsive to change."

As we traverse the dynamic terrain of personal and professional development, adaptability emerges as the superpower of the 21st century. In a world where change is constant, the ability to pivot with poise is invaluable. And we can only do this successfully and with poise when we are embedded in a culture of collaboration.

Leadership today demands more than a committed vision. Whether it is a sudden shift in market trends, a new technology breakthrough, or an unexpected turn in your personal journey, adaptability is your loyal ally. And when working as a team, we need collaboration to be able to pivot.

Consider agility and adaptability as a stimulus for growth. This challenges us to rethink, reimagine, and reinvent.

I invite you to reflect on the following:

How has adaptability played a role in your life?

_____

_____

_____

_____

_____

Have you found yourself growing through change?

_____

_____

_____

_____

_____

What are your strategies to stay resilient?

_____

_____

_____

_____

_____

As leaders, we must inspire one another to embrace the winds of change with courage and curiosity.

Remember, the path of continuous growth is paved with adaptability. Start cultivating it with your team!

Be committed to fostering agility and adaptability in your team. This will enable them to respond quickly and effectively to changing market conditions, customer needs, and competitive pressures. Create flexible structures, processes, and systems. And empower your team to make decisions with confidence and take ownership of change initiatives.

Feedback. A is a critical component of effective collaboration. It enables team members to exchange insights, perspectives, and constructive criticism to improve processes and outcomes. When individuals collaborate, they often share their work, ideas, and contributions with others. Feedback helps refine and enhance these contributions by providing valuable insights, identifying areas for improvement, and validating successful approaches.

More than just a mechanism for improvement, feedback is an essential channel of communication that fosters a sense of belonging and recognition, which are critical components for team member engagement. 360° IMPACT Leaders understand that feedback not only improves skills and processes but also significantly boosts emotional engagement and team interconnection.

At its core, feedback is an act of caring. When team leaders and colleagues collaboratively invest time in providing productive feedback, it communicates a powerful message: *"You are important to us, and so is your growth."* This emotional investment by leaders and peers helps team members feel valued and appreciated, which is fundamental to fostering a positive work environment.

The absence of feedback can make team members feel overlooked or neglected, which can lead to disengagement and a decrease in productivity.

At the beginning of my career, just like for any high-achieving emerging leader, I **_needed_** feedback! I emphasize the word "needed" because when you are young, you need some sort of compass or guiding light to tell you if you are going in the right direction. A scoreboard of some sort to indicate if you are winning or you are losing.

I had the opportunity to work with someone who served as a mentor back in my days leading teams in Stateline, Nevada. His name was Dave. A true leader. Inspiring, empathetic, no-nonsense *(my cup of tea)*, visionary and charismatic. I owe it to him to see feedback today in a positive light. When I learned to embrace feedback as a result of him being kind and specific, I was able to make that "opinion" actionable. I gained a clear understanding of how my work contributed not only to my team's success but also to the brand itself and to the overall success of providing memorable experiences for our guests. This gave me a feeling of achievement and satisfaction. He taught me at a young age that perception was everything. This alignment motivated me to do even more, to become more!

Once you start providing your team with regular, caring and thoughtful feedback, you magically stop the cycle. Your team members will stop working in silos, unaware of their performance and areas for improvement. It will encourage a culture of open communication and trust, where team members are comfortable seeking help and discussing challenges. This openness will not only enhance individual performance but also strengthen your team's dynamics. This is where team members learn to rely on one another and recognize the diverse strengths each of them brings to the table.

When you and your team members start practicing delivering feedback empathetically, it will help everyone navigate the emotional landscape of receiving "critique". It is this that reassures everyone that their contributions are being evaluated in the spirit of growth, rather than judgment. This nurtures resilience and encourages a proactive approach to problem-solving and improvement, as everyone becomes less likely to shy away from challenges and more likely to take creative and calculated risks.

Feedback provides a sense of progress and evolution. For many professionals, knowing that they are not stagnant and are evolving in their roles is a significant motivator. I know it was and continues to be for me.

The regular acknowledgment of their growth through feedback can dramatically enhance job satisfaction and loyalty to the team and organization.

Feedback is much more than a tool for guiding performance; it is a vital component of emotional engagement and team cohesion. It builds trust, nurtures a positive work culture, fosters personal growth, and ultimately, enhances team performance. All ingredients that lead to team member engagement.

By prioritizing feedback, you will empower your team to thrive not just as individual professionals but as engaged and committed members of a cohesive unit driven by mutual respect and shared goals.

Collaboration plays a pivotal role in realizing the vision of 360° IMPACT leaders who champion a culture of continuous improvement within their organizations. By fostering collaboration, these leaders create fertile ground for individuals and teams to seek out new opportunities for growth and development. Through collaborative efforts, diverse perspectives converge to spark innovative ideas and solutions. They invest in collaborative training programs, personal coaching, and mentorship initiatives that empower team members to expand their skills and knowledge. When cultivating a culture of collaboration and mutual support, 360° IMPACT leaders ensure that every individual feels valued and encouraged to contribute to the organization's growth trajectory. This is the core of continuous improvement. They recognize that continuous improvement emerges from collective efforts where collaboration fuels creativity.

Collaboration requires self-discipline. Teach your team to embrace the power of discipline to improve their ability to collaborate with others. Self-discipline is the driving force behind every story of triumph or personal breakthrough. It is not just a habit; it is a lifetime lifestyle choice that shapes the future YOU want to craft. Self-discipline in a world that constantly bombards us with instant gratification, staying focused takes more than just willpower; it takes a strategy, a daily commitment to the goal you set, and the resilience to say "no" to momentary distractions.

It is not about what you want now but what you want most.

How do you create this unwavering self-discipline for collaboration in your team? Through disciplined feedback routines and rituals.

To become a 360° IMPACT leader seeking continuous improvement powered by collaboration, I challenge you to be introspective (and do this with each of your team members as well). Ask yourself:

Where do I want to be?

_____

_____

_____

_____

What am I willing to do consistently to get there?

_____

_____

_____

_____

_____

Your life's masterpiece is in your own hands! Sculpt it with the care it deserves. You are the artist. You are the creator. And yes, you are responsible for taking YOU to where you want to be. Create a life by design!

Promoting continuous improvement requires instilling a mindset of growth and development throughout the organization. Start encouraging your team to collaboratively seek out those opportunities for enhancement and improvement. Start fostering a culture of learning, feedback, and reflection to create an environment conducive to continuous improvement.

Sustainability. Sustainable practices thrive on the foundation of collaboration, a fundamental aspect of long-term success. Collaboration mechanisms enable individuals and organizations to not only assess the immediate impact of their actions but also consider their long-term implications. This continuous loop of collaboration fosters proactive and responsive practices that adapt to evolving internal and external changes. Sustainability becomes a dynamic process, continuously refined and updated through shared insights and collective efforts.

360° IMPACT leaders excel in understanding and responding to stakeholder concerns, including employees, customers, and the community. By actively seeking collaboration from these groups, these leaders gain valuable insights into the broader impact of organizational operations on the environment and society. This collaboration forms the basis for developing strategies that mitigate negative impacts, such as waste reduction, resource conservation, and social equity enhancement.

An example of a company that has achieved success through collaborative sustainability efforts is **Unilever**. Unilever is a multinational consumer goods company that has made significant strides in embedding sustainability into its operations and supply chain practices. Unilever's *Sustainable Living Plan*, launched in 2010, is a comprehensive strategy that aims to improve the health and well-being of people, reduce environmental impact, and enhance livelihoods across its value chain. One key aspect of Unilever's success is its commitment to collaboration with various stakeholders, including suppliers, NGOs, governments, and consumers.

Through collaborative partnerships, Unilever has been able to drive innovation and implement sustainable practices throughout its supply chain. For example, Unilever collaborates with smallholder farmers to promote sustainable agriculture practices, such as water conservation and biodiversity preservation. The company also works closely with packaging suppliers to develop recyclable and biodegradable packaging materials, reducing plastic waste. Unilever's collaboration with NGOs and advocacy groups has led to initiatives like the Sustainable Palm Oil Sourcing Policy, which aims to eliminate deforestation from its palm oil supply chain.

Additionally, Unilever collaborates with consumers through campaigns and product innovations that promote sustainable living, such as promoting energy-efficient products and reducing food waste. By embracing collaboration as a core principle of its sustainability strategy, Unilever has demonstrated how collective efforts can drive meaningful change towards a more sustainable future. The company's commitment to collaboration has not only improved its environmental and social impact but has also inspired other organizations to adopt similar collaborative approaches to sustainability. This collaborative model showcases the power of partnership and shared responsibility in achieving long-term sustainability goals.

It is crucial to set ambitious sustainability goals and continuously refine them through collaboration, if we want to live in a more colorful world. By maintaining a clear vision and leveraging collaboration, leaders inspire organizations to pioneer sustainable practices with lasting impacts. Effective communication and embodiment of advocated principles inspire enthusiasm and commitment within teams, driving organizational momentum toward sustainability.

Integrating collaboration mechanisms is essential for driving sustainable change. Collaboration provides critical insights into the effectiveness of sustainability strategies, promotes transparency, and holds organizations accountable for their goals. When leveraging collaboration effectively, organizations can model practices that inspire broader adoption and enact significant environmental and social changes globally. Collaboration fuels a cascading effect of inspired and sustainable impact, fostering positive change beyond organizational boundaries.

Long-term Impact. 360° IMPACT leaders assess the long-term impact of their initiatives on stakeholders, communities, and the environment through collaborative efforts. They strive to create lasting value that extends beyond short-term gains by engaging in comprehensive assessments of their decisions and actions, considering social, environmental, social and economic factors. These leaders invest in initiatives that create shared value for stakeholders and contribute to sustainable development goals, prioritizing efforts that generate lasting positive outcomes.

Central to the ethos of 360° IMPACT is the principle of creating shared value through collaboration. 360° IMPACT leaders understand that collaborative initiatives benefiting stakeholders while contributing to broader sustainable development goals are essential for long-term success. By prioritizing collaborative efforts that drive positive change, these leaders foster a culture of responsibility and resilience within their organizations. Collaboration plays a critical role in the sustainability of initiatives led by 360° IMPACT leaders. To excel in this role, they actively seek and utilize collaborative mechanisms to inform decision-making processes and enhance impact strategies. They commit to continuous evaluation and adaptation, which are essential for maintaining alignment with evolving stakeholder needs and societal expectations.

Patagonia is a great example of an organization that has achieved long-term impact through collaboration. Their 360° IMPACT approach to sustainability put Patagonia on the map as the outdoor apparel company known for its commitment to environmental stewardship and social responsibility. Patagonia has embedded sustainability into its core business practices through initiatives such as the "Worn Wear" program, which promotes the reuse and repair of clothing to extend product lifespans and reduce waste. This initiative not only aligns with environmental goals but also fosters a community of conscious consumers who value durability and ethical production.

Patagonia collaborates extensively with stakeholders, including suppliers, NGOs, and customers, to address environmental and social challenges. For instance, the company partners with textile suppliers to develop sustainable fabrics and production processes that minimize environmental impact. Patagonia also collaborates with advocacy groups to campaign for environmental protection and sustainability policies. Their commitment to creating shared value is exemplified through initiatives like the "1% for the Planet" program, where the company donates 1% of its sales to environmental organizations worldwide. This collaborative approach not only benefits stakeholders, but also contributes to broader long-term development goals by supporting conservation efforts and community initiatives.

Another example of placing long-term impact at the forefront **MGM Resorts International**, who has been committed year after year to create a 360° IMPACT. MGM Resorts International is a global leader in entertainment, hospitality, and gaming. They recently released their annual Sustainability Report for the year 2023. This report highlights the company's commitment to sustainable practices and its efforts to create positive impacts on the environment, society, and economy.

This report showcases its progress in reducing its carbon footprint and advancing environmental sustainability across its operations. This includes initiatives such as energy efficiency improvements, waste reduction programs, and water conservation efforts. It details the expansion of renewable energy sources used, such as solar and wind power, to reduce reliance on fossil fuels and promote clean energy. It provides insights into the company's community engagement programs, philanthropic activities, and partnerships aimed at supporting local communities and fostering social well-being. It demonstrates its strong commitment to diversity and inclusion in its workforce, including initiatives to promote equality, equity, and inclusion at all levels of the organization. It provides information on initiatives focused on the health, safety, and well-being of employees, including training programs, wellness initiatives, and benefits. It highlights the company's ethical business practices, governance frameworks, and transparency in operations. The report provides detailed metrics and performance indicators, including progress against sustainability goals set by MGM Resorts International. Key performance data includes reductions in greenhouse gas emissions, waste diversion rates, water consumption metrics, and community impact assessments.

The Sustainability Report 2023 from MGM Resorts International serves as a testament to the company's ongoing dedication to long-term impact, responsible business practices, and making a meaningful difference in the communities it serves.

MGM Resorts International's long-term impact efforts play a strategic role in positioning the company within the competitive market it serves in several key ways. By prioritizing sustainability, MGM Resorts enhances its brand reputation as a responsible and forward-thinking organization. This differentiation can attract environmentally conscious customers who value ethical business practices, giving MGM a competitive edge over rivals. Increasingly, consumers prefer businesses that demonstrate commitment to sustainability. MGM's efforts can attract environmentally conscious guests who are more likely to choose a company that aligns with its values, thereby expanding its customer base.

Long-term impact also engages future generations. Employees are more likely to feel proud of their employer's efforts, leading to higher job satisfaction and reduced turnover rates.

Become a 360° IMPACT leader by leveraging collaboration not only to refine current initiatives but also to cultivate a culture of learning and improvement, to create a positive long-term impact. Embrace collaboration and empower your team to innovate and implement solutions that drive sustainable value creation.

Start exemplifying a comprehensive approach to leadership rooted in a deep commitment to creating lasting value and contributing to sustainable development. Through fostering environments where collaboration is encouraged, you will distinguish yourself as a pioneer in driving positive change within your organization and community.

And, you will be contributing to a greater impact, a 360°
IMPACT in the world.

In conclusion, the journey towards impactful leadership rooted in collaboration underscores a fundamental truth: the transformative power of collective effort.

Effective collaboration within teams not only fosters innovation and adaptation but also cultivates the resilience and agility necessary to thrive amidst change and plan a better future.

By embracing feedback as a cornerstone of growth, you will ignite a culture of continuous improvement, where every setback becomes a bridge toward progress. Inspired by visionary leaders in sustainability, we recognize that achieving lasting success is a collective effort that extends beyond organizational boundaries. It requires strategic collaboration and a commitment to shared goals for long-term impact.

As we aspire to live, lead and serve in a more colorful world, defined by collaboration, shared values, and sustainable impact, let us lead with courage and curiosity, inspiring others to join in the journey of transformative change. Together, through purposeful collaboration, we can realize lasting value, uphold ethical stewardship, and leave a profound legacy of positive change in our wake.

Your emphasis on long-term impact, shared value creation, and
collaboration-driven improvement will inspire meaningful and
enduring transformations.

Because together, everyone accomplishes more!

Key takeaways: 360° IMPACT collaboration is characterized by a combination of creating a personal board of directors, finding alignment, and being open. By embracing change and feedback, 360° IMPACT leaders can achieve sustainability and long-term impact.

BELIEF
A Powerful Force for 360° IMPACT

Unlock your potential!

When life's changes hit hard and unpredictably, there's a place of strength and renewal within us. This strength doesn't come from outside events or luck; it comes from a deep, unwavering force inside us. This force is our **belief**.

Belief quietly shapes our ability to adapt and stay strong. It's like a small ember that, even in the toughest times, can grow into a powerful flame of hope and perseverance.

In this farewell chapter, our final one *(sigh)*, I want us to take a deep dive into the very essence of human spirit and strength. I invite you to join me as we explore how belief underpins our ability to withstand life's challenges and adapt with grace to its endless ups and downs. This narrative is not merely about survival; it is about thriving. Focusing on more than just getting by or enduring challenges; it means prospering, growing, and achieving a higher level of success and well-being. It means a positive, proactive approach to life or a situation, aiming for excellence and fulfillment rather than simply avoiding failure or hardship.

It is about how, armed with belief, we transform obstacles into stepping stones and trials into triumphs.

Belief is both shield and sword in the battles we face. When the ground beneath us shifts, when we endure heartbreak, face illness, are unhappy with our job, or confront any of the myriad adversities that life throws our way, it is belief that steadies our hands and calms our hearts. It whispers in our ears that no winter lasts forever, no night so long that it can resist dawn.

Belief does not deny the existence of hardship; rather, it acknowledges the pain yet chooses to see beyond it.

Consider for a moment the raw power of belief as seen in the lives of those who have faced monumental challenges. People like Malala Yousafzai*, who, after being attacked for her advocacy of education, believed not only in her own recovery but in her continued fight for girls' education worldwide. Her resilience stems from a deep-seated belief in her cause. Or think of Nelson Mandela**, who held firm to his beliefs about justice and equality, even through 27 years of imprisonment, emerging not with bitterness but with a resolve to heal a nation.

[*Malala Yousafzai is a Pakistani female education activist and the 2014 Nobel Peace Prize laureate at the age of 17. She is the youngest Nobel Prize laureate in history, the second]

[**Nelson Rolihlahla Mandela was a South African anti-apartheid activist, politician, and statesman who served as the first president of South Africa from 1994 to 1999. He was the country's first black head of state and the first elected in a fully representative democratic election]

These stories stir something in us, do they not? They resonate because they are demonstrations of how belief can guide us through the darkest tunnels to emerge into light.

They show us that when we tether our actions to our beliefs, the impossible begins to crumble and change starts to bloom around us.

But how does belief forge such resilience and adaptability? It does so by framing our mindset, *by coloring the lenses through which we view challenges.*

When we believe that we can learn from any situation, we turn each challenge into a lesson.

When we believe that we are capable of navigating through adversity, each step we take is steadied by confidence and clarity of purpose.

Belief acts as a beacon to others, inspiring them to also stand firm in their own beliefs.

Although perhaps the most compelling aspect of belief is its role in our inner dialogues. Each of us has an ongoing narrative in our minds, a story we tell ourselves about who we are and what we are capable of achieving. Belief is the scriptwriter of this narrative. It can certainly pen a tale of doubt and limitations. But if you choose to, it can write a powerful saga of strength, resilience, and endless potential.

The stories we tell ourselves matter deeply; they can confine us or liberate us, hold us back or propel us forward. Take the example of sharing your stories of adversity with others.

Sharing your hardship not to glorify yourself, but to see how far you have come. This serves as reassurance and provides you with a bigger desire to believe in what is yet to come.

This is not just an exploration; it is a call to action! I challenge you to look inward and assess the nature of your beliefs.

- Do they lift you up?
- Do they weigh you down?
- Are they broadening your horizon, or are they fencing you in?
- Do you believe you are making an impact?
- Is it a 360° kind of impact?
- Do you believe you have the power to organize a 360° IMPACT movement?

Living a 360° IMPACT life is about breaking fences, expanding horizons, and embracing the power of belief to foster resilience and adaptability!

As you turn each page in your book of life, allow yourself to be infused with the conviction that your beliefs shape your reality. Let this understanding ignite a passion within you to cultivate beliefs that empower, that embolden, and that illuminate paths through the toughest terrains. Commit to staying inspired, to transform, and to emerge not just as someone who survives the challenges of life but as someone who thrives within them.

This is the journey of belief.

There is a lot to be said about mindset when it comes to embracing the power of belief. It serves as a transformative force. The challenge is that developing positive belief does not happen overnight. It is a journey of self-discovery, challenges, and unwavering faith. And the rewards? The rewards are immeasurable.

Neuroscience relates to beliefs by examining how different brain regions and neural processes contribute to their formation, maintenance, and modification. Beliefs are dynamic constructs shaped by experiences, information, and interactions within our environment. They act as mental frameworks that help the brain predict and understand interactions, guiding our perceptions and actions.

Beliefs are formed through neural pathways that integrate sensory information, past experiences, and cognitive processes. The prefrontal cortex plays a key role in this integration, enabling higher-order thinking and decision-making.

Once formed, beliefs are maintained through neural networks that reinforce them, often seeking consistency and confirmation, a phenomenon known as confirmation bias. The amygdala and hippocampus, involved in emotional processing and memory, further cement beliefs by linking them to emotional experiences.

Beliefs can change when new information contradicts existing beliefs or when individuals consciously engage in cognitive processes aimed at belief modification. Neuroplasticity, the brain's ability to reorganize itself by forming new neural connections, allows for the rewiring of beliefs.

So, how can we intentionally rewire our brain to believe? Here are some practices.

1. **Mindfulness and Meditation**: These practices increase awareness of existing beliefs and create mental space for new perspectives, enhancing cognitive flexibility.
2. **Cognitive Behavioral Therapy (CBT)**: CBT techniques help identify and challenge negative or limiting beliefs, replacing them with more positive ones, forming new neural pathways.
3. **Positive Reinforcement**: Engaging in positive behaviors and receiving reinforcement can help establish new beliefs by strengthening desired traits through successful experiences and feedback.
4. **Exposure to New Information and Experiences**: Seeking out diverse information and experiences can break down old beliefs and form new ones, challenging existing viewpoints.
5. **Visualization and Affirmations**: Visualization and positive affirmations can help rewire the brain by creating new neural pathways associated with positive statements and vivid mental images of achieving goals.

I absolutely love diving into the neuroscience behind beliefs because it reveals how we can truly transform our minds. By understanding how our brain works and utilizing the power of neuroplasticity, we can effectively rewire our brains to adopt new, empowering beliefs. It's fascinating to see how science gives us the tools to shape our thoughts, overcome limitations, and ultimately lead more fulfilling lives.

This reminds me of the powerful message from the show Ted Lasso* about the importance of belief. Just like Ted inspires his team to believe in themselves and each other, understanding the neuroscience behind beliefs can inspire us to make real changes fast. We can harness the power of our brains to cultivate a mindset of positivity and possibility, much like Ted encourages his team to embrace the power of belief.

[*Ted Lasso (/ˈlæsoʊ/ LASS-oh) is an American sports comedy-drama TV series created by Jason Sudeikis, Bill Lawrence, Brendan Hunt, and Joe Kelly. It follows Ted Lasso, an American college football coach hired to lead an English soccer team, whose owner hopes his inexperience will cause the team's failure. Instead, Ted's optimistic and folksy leadership brings unexpected success.]

When a positive and impactful belief takes root in your soul, the impossible starts to look possible. That is when the magic happens, doors open where there were once walls, and opportunities appear out of thin air. It is life's way of saying, *"your belief has power!"* I stand testament to this practice. I persist in coaching my clients on the importance of believing in the process, and the results have been extraordinary.

Much like Ted Lasso's optimistic and folksy leadership transforms his team's performance, in my line of work, I leverage the power of neuroscience and neuroplasticity to help clients rewire their brains and adopt empowering beliefs. An approach that highly elevates their emotional intelligence through the process. When we understand how our brains work, we can cultivate a mindset that embraces positivity and possibility, leading to real, lasting change. This is the core of my coaching philosophy—using the science of belief to understand the root cause, rewire the brain, unlock potential, and achieve remarkable success.

By believing wholeheartedly in your aspirations, you put your trust in the process that the universe, God, or whatever mighty force you hold dear to your heart, has in store for you. And you can stop worrying about the "how" or "when"!

This belief will pave the way for miraculous unfolding. Because your belief system is your strongest ally.

It is belief that fuels our passion, drives our ambition, and creates a ripple effect of positivity and success.

So, here are some enlightening questions for you to work on:

What are your beliefs (good, bad, or indifferent)?

_____

_____

_____

_____

_____

How has believing in something or someone shaped your life?

_____

_____

_____

_____

_____

Have you experienced the "magic" that unfolds after fully trusting your belief?

_____

_____

_____

_____

_____

And if you ever find yourself struggling to believe, consider this: You wouldn't plant a tree and then dig it up every few minutes to check its growth, right? So why constantly question yourself, your efforts, or your decisions? Be patient, stop overthinking, and keep watering your seed!

Thirteen years ago, when I opened my coaching and consulting firm, I embarked on a journey that transformed the very essence of who I am today as a professional and as a person. I took a leap of faith by teaching myself the power of quiet perseverance, to work diligently behind the scenes and let my achievements speak for themselves. This philosophy became the cornerstone of my business, one that not only blossomed in revenue but also in values, and most importantly in impact.

Today, I am proud to say that my venture is not just a testament to silent hard work, but a hub for meaningful and inclusive operations. It is a business that extends beyond the four walls of an office touching lives and modeling experiences for the better.

As I look back, I realize that the growth and success of my business correlate directly with a profound personal principle: believing in my own significance within the ecosystem of my enterprise. By doing so, I have been able to scale new heights inspiring more people and transforming more lives, driving a 360° IMPACT.

And the journey does not end with me. There is a universe of humans like you out there who believe. Each with a powerful story to tell and experiences of belief and stories of success to share.

You might be asking yourself: How do I teach my kids the million life lessons I have learned, so that I can save them from hardship? How can I buy the house of my dreams with this salary? How can I ensure that I remain at the heart of my business while scaling its reach and impact? How do I balance personal growth with professional expansion?.. and the list of self-doubt goes on, and on, and on, and on. These are all valid questions. Today I invite you to join an inspiring revolution of responsible, heart-led leaders that can create waves of positive change and genuine connection, through their intense BELIEF in themselves. And this can be YOU!

Never ever forget that YOU are your biggest asset, your biggest strength, and should be your biggest believer!

As the sun sets on our journey through the principles of 360° IMPACT, I hope you find yourself reflecting on the lessons shared and the transformative power of intentional growth and connection. Each chapter has unfolded a tapestry of insight, offering both guidance and inspiration for you, seeking to leave a meaningful mark on the world. Now, as we draw this narrative to a close, I urge you to consider the pivotal importance presented in this book, of connecting with one another on a higher level, one that **transcends the superficial and embraces the authentic essence of human interaction.**

The essence of this book revolves around the quality of our relationships, both personal and societal.

We stand at a crossroads where the trajectory of our impact on the world is not solely measured by the scale of our actions but by the depth of our connections.

To achieve a 360° IMPACT, we must navigate through the layers of superficiality that often obscure our genuine connections. The journey towards a more profound impact starts with recognizing the humanity in each other. Because when we connect on a deeper level, **we acknowledge the inherent dignity and worth of each individual.**

We see beyond labels and stereotypes, recognizing the rich tapestry of human experience that defines us all!

Imagine a world where every interaction is infused with empathy and understanding. Where disagreements are opportunities for dialogue rather than division. This vision is not utopian but attainable through our collective and intentional efforts to cultivate meaningful connections.

A 360° IMPACT is not confined to isolated actions but extends outward in ever-widening circles. Like ripples on a pond, our interactions have the power to create far-reaching consequences. When we connect authentically and inclusively, we inspire others to do the same, catalyzing a chain reaction of positive change.

The transformative power of a single act of kindness, a moment of genuine connection, or a conversation that bridges divides. These seemingly small gestures can have profound implications, setting in motion a cascade of impact that transcends individual actions.

Train your brain to **THINK** before; during; and after every interaction:

- Is it **T**rue?
- Is it **H**elpful?
- Is it **I**nspiring?

- Is it **Necessary**?
- Is it **K**ind?

Let us never forget that our actions today shape the legacy we leave behind. Impact is not measured in short-lived achievements but in the relationships we nurture, the communities we empower, and the lives we touch. To build a legacy of connection, we must be intentional in our efforts to bridge divides and build bridges of understanding. This requires courage and commitment, but the rewards are immeasurable, a world where empathy triumphs over apathy, where collaboration eclipses competition, and where every individual has the opportunity to thrive.

My quest to create a 360° IMPACT
ripple effect is a call to action!

An invitation to transcend the ordinary and embrace the extraordinary. I am challenging you to connect with everyone around you on a higher level. To be an agent of change and champion of empathy.

You have had an opportunity to do some serious self-reflection and learn how these concepts can be applied in your professional setting. Remember this: regardless of your role or title, if you are impacting someone, you are a leader. Choose to be a 360° IMPACT leader and start making a positive mark in the world.

I hope you close this book with a renewed sense of purpose and possibility. I hope you can commit to forging connections that transcend boundaries, using these guiding principles. Make that choice, be that changemaker, inspire, and light the way for others around you so that they can light the way for those around them. Be courageous enough to start changing lives with the power of **YOUR** 360° IMPACT!

Together, we can create a world where impact knows no bounds. A world where every interaction leaves a lasting imprint of positivity and possibility!

Let's start living, leading and serving in a more colorful world, because **humanity simply cannot wait!**

Until we meet again,
Michele

Acknowledgements

I want to extend my deepest gratitude to the extraordinary souls who have inspired me on this profound journey of writing. To my family, whose unwavering support and boundless love have been my foundation and guiding light. Your belief in me has given me the courage to embark on this creative endeavor. To my friends, colleagues and clients, whose infectious enthusiasm and endless encouragement have lifted my spirits and fueled my passion. To the mentors and teachers who have shared their wisdom and insights shaping my thoughts and nurturing my growth. To my publisher and their entire team, your guidance has been invaluable, and I am forever grateful for your belief in my words. Lastly, to the readers and supporters of this book, your interest and engagement drive me to share my voice with the world.

To you all, thank you for being a part of this journey and for inspiring me to weave words into a tapestry of meaning and emotion.

Your presence in my life is a constant source of inspiration!

About the Author

Seven-times international best-selling author Michele Kline, founded Kline Hospitality Consulting in 2010 with the purpose of helping businesses and people grow. She founded her boutique firm out of an unparalleled passion to strengthen operating procedures, enhance company culture, and focus on leadership development, in the hospitality and service industries. As the years progress and companies continue to look at injecting "hospitality" into their way of doing business, Kline Hospitality has branched out to help customer-facing businesses in various industries.

Originally from Argentina, she relocated to the United States as a young adult.

Her professional journey started in the hospitality industry from the ground, quickly moving into several high-impact positions of leadership, responsible for thousands of employees. She made her way through life by playing a game of chess. By being committed to excellence and paying close attention to those who knew more than her. With method and strategy, she took every opportunity she had to learn. From actively engaging in every project available to her involvement in boards and committees across the industry, she is continually seeking personal growth to better serve the people around her. Remarkably, she balanced these professional commitments with raising three energetic children in a loving home.

Her background helps her clients today, more than ever. She has built connections that are made available to them, gained knowledge, collected experiences, and tested many methods before she selected the best pieces of them all.

Kline Hospitality's services include coaching for organizations, which starts with an assessment of the service culture and customer service. The journey ends with a custom selection of process improvement initiatives, workshops, and group and one-on-one coaching options that meet the needs of her clients. With the objective of driving powerful conversations that lead to sustainable transformation.

Kline Hospitality provides personalized coaching and mentoring services, available in both one-on-one and group settings. In her "Connection Labs," she facilitates group sessions where individuals engage in conscious and intentional conversations, book masterminds, and retreats. These magical environments foster connections with oneself and others, introducing new concepts, ideas, and perspectives that elevate the conversation.

In her workshops, she intentionally creates memorable experiences with every interaction. By intentionally catering to all types of learners, she facilitates experiential activities enriched by purposeful conversations, group collaboration, and moments of reflection. Her presentations are enhanced with images, videos, and storytelling that resonate with individuals. Most importantly, she ensures the experience feels real and fun. The topics included in her learning catalog are critical today, as we must all *relearn to live in a better world.* We must look for ways to become the change we seek to see in our communities. Through her content, she helps elevate human behavior and build emotional intelligence.

Her coaching approach is forward-looking, emphasizing planning and accountability. She employs a holistic method, believing that all aspects of life are interconnected. By integrating priorities, clients can make better decisions. She helps clients gain clarity and equips them with tools to manage their time and energy more effectively, overcoming obstacles. These tools are designed to be lifelong resources.

Her job is to make sure her clients verbalize the life they want and help them discover the resources they have available to them. By inviting them to explore opportunities they have not thought about before. Her favorite part about working with her clients is seeing their growth. Anticipating the "aha" moments. Moments of sudden realization, inspiration, insight, recognition, or comprehension.

There is one thing that her clients have in common, it is a desire to grow. To take their leadership and communication skills to the next level, to positively impact others, and live a more integrated and meaningful life. A life with purpose!

Michele genuinely cares about the growth and success of each person she impacts. She believes in creating cultures of care where those delivering the service feel as fulfilled as those receiving it. Michele advocates for a positive mindset, ensuring that people are not trapped in a hamster wheel. Most importantly, she believes in the seamless integration of high performance, impactful leadership, strong communication, and the joy of well-being.

RECOGNITIONS:
2024 Top 15 Coaches in Las Vegas
2024 Top 30 Inspiring Women
2024 Top 40 Hospitality Podcast
2024 Top 60 Social Media Influencer
2024 Executive Coach of the Year
2023 Executive Coaching Award
2023 Most Transformative Leadership Coach in Nevada
2023 Executive Coach of the Year
2023 Women in Lodging of The Year
2022 Top 5 Coaches To Look Out For

2022 Top 35 Hospitality Podcast
2021 Global Top 15 Trainers in Hospitality
2018 Learning & Development Professional of the Year

www.klinehospitality.com

Ready to take your personal and professional growth to the next level? Consider <u>individual coaching sessions</u> tailored to **explore the topic of balance and effective communication in-depth.** Together, we can unlock your full potential and create a more balanced, harmonious world.

Wishing you balance and positivity in all your endeavors!

Let's <u>schedule a call</u> to talk about how my coaching approach can accelerate your growth and that of your team!

Michèle Kline

Leadership & Performance Certified Coach

Leading with passion